THE PRIESTHOOD OF THE FAITHFUL

Key to a Living Church

Paul J. Philibert, O.P.

LITURGICAL PRESS
Collegeville, Minnesota

www.litpress.org

1   2   3   4   5   6   7   8

Library of Congress Cataloging-in-Publication Data

Philibert, Paul J.
    The priesthood of the faithful : key to a living church / by Paul J. Philibert.
      p. cm.
    Summary: "Explores the doctrine of the priesthood of the baptized and examines its significance for the spiritual growth of the faithful and the revitali-zation of the church"—Provided by publisher.
    Includes bibliographical references and index.
    ISBN-10: 0-8146-3023-5 (pbk. : alk. paper)
    ISBN-13: 978-0-8146-3023-5 (pbk. : alk. paper)
    1. Priesthood, Universal. I. Title.

BT767.5.P48 2005
234—dc22   2005002928

In grateful tribute to
Marie-Dominique Chenu, O.P.
and Christian Duquoc, O.P.
who taught me
to love real questions
in theology

Contents

Acknowledgments   vii

1. A Timely Discussion   1
2. Chosen to Live   22
3. Living, Holy Signs   39
4. A Priesthood Embracing Christ's Body   56
5. People Who Speak for the Spirit   74
6. Hearts Set on the Kingdom of God   93
7. Lives Lifted in Praise   113
8. An Intentional Symbolic Life   132

Appendix A: Graced Sign and Realized Mystery   158
Appendix B: An Open Letter to Religious   164
Index of Names   170
Index of Subjects   172

Acknowledgments

Completing this book is the realization of a cherished dream. For years I have nourished the idea of laying out the theological foundations for the apostolic mandate of the faithful and of their call to holiness in terms accessible to earnest lay readers. Yves Congar had already done this years ago in his classic volume *Lay People in the Church*. But much theological ground has been covered since the 1950s when he published that book, most particularly the theological developments of the Second Vatican Council and forty years of pastoral practice influenced by that council. Over quite a few years, my Dominican colleague, Gerard Austin, helped me keep the flame of this interest alive with conversations on this topic, and not a few of my perspectives expressed here owe their inspiration to my conversations with him.

I owe many debts of gratitude incurred in the process of pulling this project together. My religious order gave me the freedom to spend a sabbatical year at work on this project, and I must thank the Provincial of the Southern Dominican Province, the Very Reverend Martin J. Gleeson, O.P., for his permission and encouragement. In addition, Mepkin Abbey received me for the academic year 2003–2004 as a theologian in residence and as a visiting member of their Trappist community. I am immensely grateful to the monks of Mepkin and to their Abbot, the Right Reverend Francis Kline, O.C.S.O., for a warm and fraternal welcome and a year of common life that will deeply mark the rest of my days. The monks of Mepkin patiently listened to portions of the manuscript in a number of chapter talks. The librarian of the Clare Boothe Luce Library at Mepkin, Annette H. Nielsen, was very helpful and offered much friendly support through the year.

A number of friends and colleagues have been generous in helping me to revise or rethink my manuscript. Professor Zeni Fox of Immaculate Conception Seminary generously read and commented on an early draft of the book. Patrick Marrin, editor of *Celebration*, accompanied me in the writing process with his comments and his friendship. Daniel Lizárraga, Terri Garza, and Virgilio Elizondo each assisted me to reconsider the remarks I made concerning Catholic Latinos. Kathleen Norris read some early chapters and offered helpful suggestions.

A very special appreciation is due to Susan Carozza and Cecilia Wilkinson Enns for their intense investment in this project. Both of them agreed to read my manuscript with a critical eye, and both gave me treasured insights and important improvements.

Susan is the mother of four children, wife of a Law Professor named Paolo, and an active parish leader who is passionately enthusiastic about the grace of Christian family life. Her love of the Church caught me up short several times when, from my meager experience of actual parish life, I spoke without sufficient appreciation for the life-giving dynamics of parish communities.

Cecilia is the mother of two teenagers and the wife of an agricultural researcher named John. A writer herself, she brought an editor's eye and a wealth of theological understanding to her thorough dossier of revisions to my first draft. Her avid hopes to reach folks in the pews made for generous assistance beyond my dreams. The voices of both these terrific friends are clearly present in their contributions to my manuscript. It would not be the pastoral message that I hope it is without their rich contributions. I must acknowledge Cecilia Wilkinson Enns as the de facto editor of my manuscript. (Thanks are due to Paolo and John as well, who put up with Susan and Cecilia as they labored on my behalf.)

Finally, I want to express my thanks to Reverend Charles E. Bouchard, O.P., President of Aquinas Institute of Theology in St. Louis, who offered me various privileges as Distinguished Visiting Professor of Church and Society at Aquinas for the last several years, including during this sabbatical year. I often had the faculty and students of this excellent school of theology and pastoral ministry in mind as I wrote about the ecclesiology of a collaborative Church for this book. Their colleagueship and friendship have been a blessing.

Mepkin Abbey
Feast of Saint Augustine, 2004

Chapter 1

A Timely Discussion

Catholic theology has been neglecting an important, potentially central, doctrine of the church that is clearly articulated in the New Testament, in the documents of Vatican II, and in the Catechism of the Catholic Church. I believe that now is the time to retrieve this doctrine and explore its potential to heal a wounded church. What is this important doctrine? Look at the following texts:

> Like living stones, let yourselves be built into a spiritual house, to be a holy priesthood, to offer spiritual sacrifices acceptable to God through Jesus Christ (1 Pet 2:5).

> The baptized, by regeneration and the anointing of the Holy Spirit, are consecrated as a spiritual house and a holy priesthood, that through all their Christian activities they may offer spiritual sacrifices and proclaim the marvels of him who has called them out of darkness into his wonderful light (The Dogmatic Constitution on the Church, n. 10).

> The whole community of believers is, as such, priestly. The faithful exercise their baptismal priesthood through their participation, each according to [their] own vocation, in Christ's mission as priest, prophet, and king. Through the sacraments of Baptism and Confirmation the faithful are "consecrated to be . . . a holy priesthood" (*Catechism of the Catholic Church*, n. 1545).

This priesthood of the *totus Christus*—the whole Christ, head and members—is not about a historical sacrifice in the past alone, but also about the living sacrifices of Christ's members joined to him in faith and the Holy Spirit. The ordinary actions of their daily life become the very essence of the offering that the faithful make to God along with Christ's sacrifice. It will require careful and patient explanation for us to flesh-out all the meanings of this profound mystery. But this biblical truth stands at the center of our Christian life.

We start by examining the sense of destiny this holy teaching offers today's Christians, as well as the cultural and social reasons why baptismal priesthood provides a new grasp on life for the church today. Let us begin with a powerful call from the apostle Paul to realize the priestly nature of our Christian existence.

SCRIPTURE'S APPEAL TO UNDERSTAND AND LIVE A PRIESTLY EXISTENCE

"I appeal to you therefore, brothers and sisters, by the mercies of God, to present your bodies as a living sacrifice, holy and acceptable to God, which is your spiritual worship" (Rom 12:1). With these words, Paul reaps the harvest of his theology of life in the Spirit in the letter to the Romans. We will see what that theology is all about as we gradually review the key themes concerning the meaning of the Christian life in the New Testament letters of the apostle Paul.

Christians are transformed, Paul tells us, by two life-changing, divine gifts: faith and the Holy Spirit. By faith and through the action of the Spirit, a disciple becomes a new being so profoundly united with Christ as to form one body with him: "So we, who are many, are one body in Christ, and individually we are members one of another" (Rom 12:5-6). Once we understand God's plan, we can see that our lives are part of a bigger picture, and that they are also strategic for the realization of God's purposes. In fact, we do not "belong" to ourselves. St. Paul is quite clear: "We do not live to ourselves, and we do not die to ourselves . . . . we are the Lord's"(Rom 14:7, 8). Our decisions and our actions are never exclusively our individual concern. Everything we do has an impact upon who we become, and therefore a consequent impact upon our readiness to manifest the authentic values of the Body of Christ.

This powerful vision of human transformation has been the source of renewal in the church many times through the course of the centuries. When Martin Luther began lecturing on Paul's letters to the Romans and the Galatians, at the University of Wittenberg about the year 1515, he found in Paul's teaching about the gift of the Holy Spirit his understanding of the sheer grace of justification. He grasped that God has given us in Christ a new starting point—a new Adam, whose obedience wipes out the curse of sin inherited from our first parents and establishes a dominion of grace leading to eternal life.

Luther was overwhelmed by the gratuity and the generosity of God's gift to us in Christ, and he insisted that this doctrine superseded all the conventional theology of his time. For him, justification in Christ meant lifting a grim burden of blind legalism to make possible a new life of joyful spontaneity in the power of faith and the Holy Spirit. For centuries, Roman Catholics dismissed Luther as a troubled and dangerous heretic. But many Catholic theologians today consider Luther as a thoughtful resource for the growth in faith of the entire church. For more than three decades, there have been official international and North American Catholic-Lutheran dialogues that acknowledge the stimulus for renewal of Luther's grasp of the divine gift of Christian life in the Holy Spirit.

Paul's doctrine of life in the Spirit was also the foundation for the charismatic renewal of the late 1960s. Many contemporary Christians understood for the first time the transforming nature of divine faith and the reality of the gifts of the Holy Spirit through their participation in charismatic Scripture study and prayer groups. Clearly this is a doctrine that has the potential to change lives. The charismatic renewal never became a dominant force in the twentieth century, but it did lead many Christians to move their faith from the periphery to the center of their lives.

This same doctrine about human lives transformed by faith and by the gift of the Holy Spirit is also at the heart of the book you are about to begin reading. We will take this teaching one step further and show how the Christian spiritual life is oriented toward believers joining their lives to Christ's sacrificial and redeeming life. We Catholics are not accustomed to calling our daily activities the "obedience of faith" or an expression of "priesthood." But we need to learn this way of speaking (and living), since it is the tradition of God's revelation. Further, it is very apt at this moment in the life of a troubled church for the baptized to accept their call to a priestly and transforming presence in the world. Before explaining more fully the doctrine of baptismal priesthood, which will come in the following chapters, I want to make the argument that this is a very timely discussion for the Church to have.

In the opening lines of Romans 12, cited above, Paul speaks with urgency as if to say "Please wake up! Recognize that the meaning of your life is to offer yourselves and all you do to become part of God's own project of saving and claiming creation for eternal life." In his phrase, "present your bodies," Paul means your whole selves. Paul's use of the Greek word, *soma*, refers to the whole person—body and soul—understood as a vital unity. When Paul uses the phrase "living sacrifice," he is referring to the willing, intentional reinvestment that Christians make when they shape their lives no longer by immediate material interests, but rather by their confidence in the gift of future resurrection, what Paul calls "newness of life." Our energies and actions, redirected by Christ's Spirit, reach out to touch and convert the world around us.[1]

The following powerful lines of Romans 8:19 are well known: "For the creation waits with eager longing for the revealing of the children of God . . . in hope that the creation itself will be set free from its bondage to decay and will obtain the freedom of the glory of the children of God." All the baptized are these "children of God," members of Christ's body, and agents of the new creation. It does not matter what their context is—rich or poor, mighty or humble, sophisticated or simple, public or domestic. Each baptized person living in the Spirit of Jesus is an instrument whom God has claimed for the work of directing the world and its energies to the glory of God and the joy of God's friendship.

This vision can appeal to the idealism and hope of people in any culture and any generation. Perhaps it touches hearts more powerfully in contexts of poverty, exile, suffering, or injustice. Without question, St. Paul meant it to be an invitation to a new life and a new world. Blessed are those who know their need of God.

We continue to proclaim these words year after year and season after season in the church. So what, then, is the explanation for the minimal impact of this transforming Christian vision upon Christians today and upon our Christian communities? Archbishop Sean O'Malley of Boston recently reported that one of his pastors responded to his question about how many people his church holds by saying, "Bishop, my church sleeps seven hundred."[2] There are churches all over our land that sleep seven hundred and more on Sunday mornings when the people gathered for Mass find no link between their lives and their worship. The Christian vision of Paul has only minimal impact when the sickness, sacrifices, and unselfishness of the faithful are lived out with no awareness that those dimensions of their lives are at the heart of their Christian priesthood. How can people be awakened to the real meaning of becoming Christians? This question about the impact of the Good News is a good place to begin framing the church's teaching about the priestly life of baptized disciples of Christ.

A CRITICAL MOMENT

Shortly after the passage in Romans 12, which we have just examined, Paul appeals to his readers to understand that his proclamation of the new creation through faith and the Holy Spirit is of critical importance. They may not have comprehended before the importance of their call to faith and discipleship or the difference that their lives can make in liberating a world burdened with violence and injustice. But now that they have grasped the real significance of their lives on earth, they can no longer afford to ignore its implications. Life in Christ is not one among many meanings that shape their lives; it is *the* meaning of their life.

Paul says, "you know what time it is, how it is now the moment for you to wake from sleep. For salvation is nearer to us now than when we became believers . . ." (Rom 13:11). Such a call to attention and alertness is sometimes referred to as a moment of *kairos*—a Greek word used by Paul in his letters that speaks of a time for decision, a time when we perceive everything in a new way. This word is central to what Paul wants us to understand, namely, that because of the awakening of faith we have begun a new life dating from the moment of our first believing. We will be returning to the idea of *kairos*. It means a time when we come to perceive everything in a new way.

Most people would agree that the North American church is presently at a moment of *kairos*. Many concerned Catholics feel that we can no longer go about business as usual. Groups like Voice of the Faithful (which we will discuss later in this chapter) have been formed in many cities now by people who want to have a say in how the Catholic community presents itself to the world. This is a perfect example of the faithful taking responsibility to be public witnesses to their faith. It appears controversial to those who are not accustomed to an apostolic laity. But the numbers of people who fear the faithful taking an active role in the Church's public life will decrease in time.

Many active and dedicated Catholics are refusing to be passive any longer. Their concerns are not expressions of despair or negativity. Rather, they see that the U.S. church today is faced with a moment of extraordinary opportunity. The crisis of sexual abuse has awakened within many Catholics a sense of responsibility for the Church that they previously did not feel. Let us look for a moment at some of the most obvious characteristics of our current predicament.

GROWING NUMBERS, FEWER PRIESTS

Numerically, the Catholic Church in the U.S. is growing rapidly. The 2000 CARA Report, *Catholicism Today*, puts it rather dramatically: in the year 1900 one out of seven Americans was Catholic (11 million in a population of 76 million). Today more than one in five Americans is at least nominally Catholic (60 million in a population of 267 million). The factors that account for this demographic development include the impact of immigration, intermarriage leading to adult reception of spouses into the Catholic Church, and, of course, natural increase through family growth. All of these factors have made the Catholic Church the largest single denomination in what was for two centuries a dominantly Protestant country.[3]

Who ministers to this growing Catholic population? The simplest answer today is too few priests. Many dioceses, particularly those in the upper Midwest, are experiencing a marked decrease in the availability of ordained pastors. The number of parishes without a resident pastor has grown to over 3,150 nationwide. More than seventeen percent of U.S. parishes are entrusted to the administration of a nonresident pastor or to someone other than a priest.[4] Particularly in the Midwest, the pairing and clustering of parishes is a frequent response to the shortage of priests. Two or three rural parishes are often served by a single pastor. This can be disappointing for the parishioners and quickly exhaust the pastors, especially when pastors must serve parishes in several distinct towns or distant rural areas.

Given the Church's official position on qualifications for ordained ministry, the strategy most commonly used by U.S. bishops to remedy this shortage has been to seek foreign-born priests to come to U.S. dioceses to assist the bishops in diocesan ministry. (This has long been a formula used in clergy-poor dioceses, as witnessed by the large number of foreign-born Irish pastors in many southern dioceses.) Such large, influential dioceses as Chicago and Baltimore have announced distinct policies to recruit priests from abroad to be brought in as pastors. And some seminaries have begun special programs to prepare foreign-born priests to enter effectively into American culture and society. A national study is currently being conducted on foreign-born priests in the U.S. church, and initial indications are that nearly twenty percent of priests currently serving in U.S. parishes are now foreign-born.[5]

The pastoral need is real. The generosity on the part of these foreign missionaries to the U.S. church is notable. However, the results are sometimes disappointing as in those cases in which a foreign-born missionary in a U.S. parish has difficulty in pronouncing English clearly or, even more serious, when he fails to appreciate the collaborative spirit of ministry in the U.S. church and ends up destroying the cooperative lay supports for ministry that pre-existed his arrival. There are, of course, many parishes where there has never been much collaboration or support for lay activism.

There are many tensions connected with the clergy shortage. The fatigue and discouragement of our native-born priests themselves is a factor that is likely to increase as the largest cohort of U.S. priests ever ordained—those ordained between 1948 and 1958—disappears from ministry through retirement, illness, or death. Today about two-thirds of our diocesan priests are over the age of fifty-five; thirty-seven percent are over the age of sixty-five. Fewer than twenty percent are under the age of forty-five.[6]

Many Catholics in vital, community-centered parishes are frustrated when their bishops are unable to assure future leadership that will sustain the collaborative and comprehensive style of ministry to which they have become accustomed. William D'Antonio, a distinguished sociologist at Catholic University in Washington, summarizes lay attitudes by saying that, "it is clear that the laity wants to retain strong parishes and priestly services and welcomes new administrative arrangements and expansion of priestly roles in order to do so."[7] The laity are not opposed to seeing priests share some of their pastoral roles with the faithful.

On the other hand, at the same time that this shortage of ordained ministers is causing concern and stress, church life in North America is blessed with a growing number of gifted lay ecclesial ministers working in parish and diocesan roles. Approximately thirty-thousand of these laypersons are active in a range of ministries such as pastoral coordinator, religious education, liturgy, youth ministry, and many other ministries dealing with relationships both inside and outside the parish. In addition, more than thirty thousand laypersons are currently enrolled in diocesan, seminary, and university programs of formation for ministry. The number of lay ministers is increasing, and the number of parishes employing them is increasing as well. Approximately two-thirds of all U.S. parishes currently employ Lay Ecclesial Ministers.[8]

Such ministerial roles are open to all lay persons, but in fact women provide eighty percent of the workforce in the church today.

A fourth of these are religious sisters. Among the male and female ministers who are not religious, about two-thirds are married persons. The average age of U.S. lay ministers is fifty, whereas the average age of priests is over sixty. On the whole, lay ministers are well educated, although their formal education and degrees may be unrelated to the religious or pastoral work that they do. Eighty percent of them are college educated and more than fifty percent have at least a master's degree.[9] However, many of those degrees are not in competencies for theology, ministry, or social service. Nonetheless, a tradition of lay ecclesial ministry is evolving that will change the face of the U.S. church.

The *kairos* dimension of this story has to do with the understanding of leadership that is implicit in church policies. Our current situation, which includes growing church ministries and diminished numbers of the ordained, demonstrates the reasonableness of the apostolic action of the baptized as a priestly people. The theology of baptismal priesthood has the capacity to change our view of the current ministry crisis. A possible benefit of this crisis may be a renewed recognition of the priestly character of all Christians and a wider acceptance of their responsibility for the life of the Church. This will not put ordained priests out of the picture; rather, it will clarify how Christ's priesthood transforms the world and its social structures through the apostolic action of the people of God. Such a clarification will help to shape the pastoral mission of the ordained as well, as we shall see.

A LOSS OF CONNECTIONS

In this growing U.S. Catholic Church, other forces of change are also at work. This is perceptible in terms of the Mass attendance of Catholics. Statistics indicate a continuing decline in Mass attendance, and a dangerous alienation of young adults and minority populations in particular. It is important to figure out why this is happening.

In the 1940s and 1950s, approximately three-quarters of the U.S. Catholic population attended Sunday Mass every week. Throughout the 1960s and 70s, the percentage of Catholics going to weekly Mass declined steadily. Data from the late 1990s and the year 2000 show that weekly Mass attendance has dropped to somewhere around thirty-five percent, and some researchers suggest that it may be even lower. CARA research estimates that around eighteen million Catholics attend Mass on a typical weekend.[10] By this they mean thirty percent of those Catholics registered in parishes; if viewed as a percentage of total U.S. Catholics, that percentage would be approximately twenty-seven percent.

About forty percent of Catholics attend Mass only a few times a year. However, when we isolate the population of Catholic young adults, the data show only twenty-one percent of them attending Mass weekly. A huge forty-nine percent of young adults fall into the category of Mass attendance a few times a year.[11] This puts the majority of those who call themselves Catholics in a somewhat tenuous relationship to the life of the Catholic Church.

What are the reasons offered by researchers for this significant shift in participation in the Church's sacramental life? Sociologists offer several explanations. First, half a century of Catholics' assimilation into the individualism of U.S. culture is eroding their compliance with church law. They have adopted a dominantly internal locus of authority, that is, decision-making based on personal judgment, which leaves them more room for choice. Furthermore, since Vatican II, bishops and priests have stressed obligation less as a motive for attending Mass, and put more emphasis on a personal decision to attend.

Lay Catholics have been given the responsibility to choose to attend, but have not been given sufficient explanation about the values and benefits of regular attendance. Beyond that, Pope Paul VI's 1968 encyclical *Humanae Vitae*, banning artificial birth control, has contributed to lay Catholics' loss of confidence in the church's authority.[12] This has affected negatively their sense of the importance of the church in their lives. Some Catholics feel so distant from the church's moral teaching that they can only come to Sunday Eucharist with resentment or a divided heart.

Other reasons include social and environmental factors, such as the decline of anti-Catholic prejudice in public life across the span of the twentieth century (and the consequent loss of Catholic "let's-hang-together" solidarity), the loss of tightly knit urban Catholic neighborhoods, and the growth of mixed marriages. Various research reports place the frequency of Catholics in mixed marriages somewhere between a third and a half of them. All of the research, however, interprets the growth of mixed marriages as a major factor in the loss of the affiliation of young adults with the church because of the tensions between the spouses based on their loyalties to their churches of origin or on their different degrees of religiosity.[13]

Closer to home, it is clear that parents are worn out by Sunday morning, and Mass seems like a choice rather than an obligation. Parents who do not see much of their children during the work week are now more likely to give in to children's desires about what they do when they are together. So the parents are less likely to take the family to Mass against the wishes of their child. Children—especially those who are in travel sports or high school sports—often have sporting activities that destroy the sense of Sunday as Sabbath or a family day. Another factor may be the current idea that people can "parish hop." If they are dissatisfied with their local parish, they tend to lose any sense of urgency about needing weekly spiritual care. The question, "Where are we going this week, dear?" is not a highly motivating encouragement to understand the family's active role in building the parish community.

For present purposes, these data and their interpretation suggest an evident need for an evangelistic or missionary posture on the part of bishops and pastors. On the one hand, Catholics still believe in God and love their Church, and most cannot imagine joining another denomination. *The Search for Common Ground*, James Davidson's study just cited, clearly shows this to be the case. But on the other hand, many Catholics seem to have lost a sense of urgency both about needing weekly spiritual care and about the importance of contributing in a significant way to the life of the church.

Young adult Catholics especially have become distanced from regular church attendance and are no longer rooted in the parish community. The picture that emerges here is a consumer-oriented model of Catholic spiritual life. The parish functions as a spiritual commodity available every Sunday for those who are so inclined. This being the case, it appears the majority of Catholics feel like they need a sleep-in, a game of golf, or a quiet morning with the newspaper more than they need Sunday Mass.

James Davidson and his colleagues have summarized the factors that seem to influence why people become disaffiliated or alienated from the church. People with little religious formation as children will feel that religion is not an important part of life; such a profile predicts their dropping out. If parents are not on fire with faith, then it is likely that their children too will be less than committed. In addition, when people get caught up in family traumas like separation, divorce, or the death of a spouse, and fail to find much support from their fellow parishioners, they frequently turn away from church.

Low education, poor jobs, and low income are also conditions that foster dropping out. Some people, these sociologists suggest, are too embarrassed to register in the parish because they cannot afford to contribute. African Americans and Latino Catholics sometimes find themselves treated differently because of their race and ethnicity, and feel turned off. In the years of massive immigration between 1890 and 1930, many ethnic communities held on to their faith because it provided a strong social framework in urban areas. Today things are very different. Most immigrants do not find a culturally friendly, language-matched parish to support them.

Single young people commonly stop attending church almost as a matter of course. Davidson calls this adolescent dropping out "almost a rite of passage," as they experiment with life without church once they are out of reach of parental supervision. The church becomes sidelined by their search for a profession, their efforts to get ahead, and their quest for a spouse. The church and Christian faith seem to be irrelevant in these questions because we haven't been taught well about vocation, mission, and the life of grace. And finally there are those married to non-Catholics, which is a growing population, as we just noted.[14]

If there is a *kairos* element here, it seems to me, it is the need for large numbers of nominal Catholics, such as those we have just discussed, to be formed in an adult faith that can transform their view of the Church as provider of spiritual commodities, and themselves as spiritual consumers. Spiritual materialism or consumerism is a threat to any spiritual tradition. A charismatic Buddhist teacher some years ago wrote a successful little book entitled *Cutting Through Spiritual Materialism*[15] in which he argued that truth, not personal satisfaction, is the focus of spirituality. At bottom, the purpose of Christian faith and life is not to satisfy the curiosity or appetites of believers, but to recruit them into the action of God's Spirit in building the kingdom of God.

Faith and the Christian life introduce a person into what St. Paul calls a "new creation"—a new kind of life and relationship to the world that entails spiritual growth for the sake of the world's salvation. This is another way of describing the priesthood of the baptized, and we will show in the following chapters how grasping this transforms one's understanding of worship, community, and sense of responsibility. Without this kind of understanding, religion too easily remains a take-it-or-leave-it commodity.

LATINO CHRISTIANS LOOKING FOR LIFE

The fastest growing segment of the changing U.S. church is the Hispanic/Latino population. Demographers estimate their numbers to be close to twenty percent of U.S. Catholics. Their proportion to the local Catholic population varies considerably from place to place. In certain dioceses, they are the dominant Catholic presence. For instance, Latino Catholics make up more than fifty percent of the Catholic population of the two states of Texas and New Mexico, one-third of California and Arizona, and one fourth of Catholics in Colorado and Florida.[16] While the number of Latinos is growing both in the U.S. population and in the Catholic Church here, it is also clear that the number of Latinos who identify themselves as Catholic is decreasing. The CARA 2000 survey claims that just over half of U.S. Latinos consider themselves Catholic. Thus the future growth of Latino presence in the general U.S. population will be larger than the growth of Latinos in Catholic dioceses and parishes.

Some sense of the significance of these statistics can be measured by looking at Latino scholars in church-related academic life. For every Latino Catholic in a U.S. seminary preparing for ordination, there are three Latino Protestants in U.S. seminaries preparing for ordained ministry. Various factors weigh in here. Church law has it that candidates for Catholic priestly ordination are required to be male and celibate. In contrast, Protestant candidates for ordained ministry may be female and married. Additionally, the Catholic program for priestly education and formation is highly structured and academic. It presupposes completion of secondary, undergraduate, and some graduate education, while many Protestant seminaries or denominations are willing to accommodate their ministry formation programs to the individual needs of zealous candidates who may lack a conventional academic background. There is reason to believe that, as a result of these differences in recruitment and pastoral formation, Protestant denominations are drawing upon the natural leaders of many Latino communities to a greater degree than are Catholic dioceses.[17]

The situation in graduate programs of religious studies and theology is similar to that in seminaries. As a conservative guess, I would judge that, for every Catholic Latino graduate student in doctoral level studies in religion or theology, there are two or three Protestant Latino graduate students. I am basing this guess on the research proposals that I have received over the past six years as a member of the Board of the Louisville Institute, one of the principal foundations funding individual religious research projects for U.S. Christian denominations. There are decidedly more Protestant Latino sociologists, pastoral theologians, and historians in the U.S. studying Latino culture than there are Catholics in these categories.

Frequently this results in Latino Protestant lay scholars appropriating historical, cultural, social, and theological traditions that have strong Roman Catholic roots. Careful research would be needed to identify the motivation of and support for these lay Protestant vocations to religious scholarship. However, there are two apparent consequences of this situation: much of the intellectual aristocracy of American Latino Christianity has been recruited to work in Protestant intellectual circles and, additionally, traditional Roman Catholic cultural and theological themes (such as Liberation Theology) are being appropriated by Protestant intellectuals and pastors. The point here is not one of jealousy about Protestant successes in fostering the talent of former Roman Catholics; rather, the point is to bring attention to the missed opportunities of Catholic institutions to nurture a Latino population too long taken for granted.[18]

It has been long supposed that Latin Americans are Catholic by tradition and cultural identity. Today, however, we find strong challenges to the continuing identification of Latinos with their Catholic heritage. Writing in 1984, John Blackall describes the effects of Protestant proselytizing in the Southwest: "Texas has over a million Hispanic Baptists. . . . The Atlanta based Southern Baptist Convention has 1,500 Hispanic churches and adds 150 a year. The Jehovah's Witnesses, based in Brooklyn, New York, have 45,000 Hispanic members and the number is steadily increasing. The American Lutheran Church's Commission on Hispanic Ministries is into a ten-year project to support and train personnel for Hispanics in the U.S."[19]

What is the attraction here? Nancy Bedford, an American Protestant seminary professor in Argentina who pastors a church in Buenos Aires has written an article recently describing the attraction of Protestant church life for former Roman Catholics in Latin America. "Nominal" Roman Catholics, she says, have been attracted to an active evangelical faith through Bible education, individual invitations into welcoming and strongly personal small communities of worship, and the church's involvement in their family and workplace concerns.

According to Nancy Bedford, "Latin American religiosity, Christian and non-Christian, is highly complex. Sociologists are presently struggling to find a proper nomenclature to describe the various

non-Roman Catholic Christian faith groups that are gaining influence
. . . particularly within the poorest sectors of society. Recent studies
illustrate the extent to which Roman Catholicism has lost its monop-
oly of symbolic goods . . . and the high growth rates of Protes-
tantism and Afro-Brazilian religions, such as *umbanda*, among the
poor."[20] Further, we should note that in Latin America in many
people's minds the Catholic Church is associated with oppressive political regimes.

Such sociologists as James Davidson and his colleagues have urged
the U.S. Catholic hierarchy to respond to this decline in Latino
Catholicity with very strong measures for evangelization. But this
brings us face to face again with the question of the decreasing number of Catholic clergy. They are, as we noted above, very often
stretched by overwork and in danger of burning out. In a *National
Catholic Reporter* study about the priest shortage, Auxiliary Bishop
Thomas Curry of Los Angeles remarked that immigration has aug-
mented the population of some of his parishes to eighteen thousand
households. He went on to say that if we really were to emphasize
reaching out to dormant Catholics in situations like that, it would be
hard to say what the results might be. In his words, "If we invite
them back, what in heaven's name will we do with them?"[21]

The promise and challenge of the growing Latino church in the
U.S. is surely a *kairos* moment. Typically Latino Catholicism locates
the religious center of gravity inside the family rather than inside the
parish church. Latino Catholics are deeply attracted to popular expressions of religion, such as devotion to our Lady of Guadalupe, domestic altars, and family celebrations at which parents—often the
mother—preside. By contrast, in too many situations, our bishops
and pastors have expected Latino Catholic immigrants to move with
docility from small parish communities to huge urban ones, and from
a religious atmosphere based in popular devotion to an astringently
spare liturgical life. Beyond that, most Latino immigrants are obliged
to shift from Spanish language and Latino piety to English language
and Anglo efficiency. All this comes as a rude awakening, given their
religious culture.

The challenge raised by this interface of Hispanic romanticism and
Anglo pragmatism provides yet another warrant to explore the mediating role of the Church's teaching about the priesthood of the baptized. This theology has a place for the religious significance and
theological power of domestic ritual and popular religiosity. In tech-

nically non-liturgical acts of worship, it is the baptized who preside over the priestly actions that can bind families together, celebrate the communal joy of neighborhoods, and center traditional Latino lives once again back in the heart of the church.

When the church helps Latino and other Catholic immigrants, like the new wave of Asian and Pacific Island Catholics recently arrived in our country, explore the nurturing and evangelizing potential of their traditions of popular religiosity, it welcomes them and their cultural heritage as new people in its midst. But it is also enriching its common ecclesial life. The evidence is clear that the church needs to increase the temperature of the Anglo Catholic parish experience if it is going to enhance its attractiveness to a new generation. This can clearly become a win-win situation if we have the courage and the imagination to attend to the possibilities.

RECONSIDERING OUR DIGNITY AS A GIFTED PEOPLE OF GOD

It would be a mistake to ignore the sexual-abuse scandal in the U.S. Catholic Church, as this contributes to the dynamic of the church's present moment of *kairos*. The media's ruthless pursuit of incidents related to the abuse crisis has affected not only the bishops and clergy, but the whole church. All this notoriety has diminished the church's moral authority and become the occasion for mortifying embarrassment and fear on the part of both clergy and laity alike.

Attorney Patrick Schiltz has summarized the fundamental issue as succinctly as possible, I think, where he writes: "Hundreds of pastors . . . did indeed sexually abuse thousands of children and vulnerable adults. Many bishops and other church leaders did indeed learn of abusive pastors, cover-up abuse, and do little to protect children and vulnerable adults."[22] As a consequence, Catholic dioceses have spent hundreds of millions of dollars combating clergy sexual misconduct. This has been terribly costly, and in an already bad economy, the costs of litigation and settlements have caused dioceses to further reduce the services they provide. Schiltz points out the irony that, "[T]his is the first time in history in which punitive damages are being inflicted upon the victims—or at least those completely innocent—of wrongful conduct."[23] By this he means that the most vulnerable elements in our urban societies will be the ones to pay the most for these damages by way of eliminated social programs and services. The innocent will end up paying for the wrongs of the guilty.

Another consequence of this crisis has been the emergence among lay Catholics of a determination to demand both greater accountability from their bishops for their actions and some meaningful role for the laity in local church governance. In January 2002, in a Catholic parish in the Boston suburb of Wellesley, Dr. Jim Muller assembled the first gathering of a group calling itself Voice of the Faithful. Muller has explained his motivation by saying: "This scandal awakened me to [some] terrible flaws in our church. I reached the painful conclusion that I must either attempt to correct these deep structural defects or leave the Catholic Church."[24] Muller describes the problem as "a concentration of power in the hierarchy—as though the executive, legislative and judicial branches were combined." Many of the laity have long felt unjustly deprived of a meaningful voice in the church's decision making. However, the events of the past several years have pushed some of them over the line that divides passivity from concerned response.

Since late antiquity, the Roman Catholic Church has developed the tendency to segregate its members into a hierarchy, on the one hand, and the laity, on the other hand. This means a division between sanctifiers and sanctified, holy and sinful, essential and peripheral. This clericalized version of Catholic Christianity identifies the church's holiness and transformative power with the rites of liturgical celebrations, and not with the Christian transformation of families, cities, work, and culture. In this view, as long as the hierarchy is there to celebrate the sacraments, the church is functioning properly. At its worst, this clerical attitude simply dismisses the complaints, interests, or initiatives of the non-ordained as unenlightened or irrelevant. The clear identification of the church with the full community of the baptized will always need to be the object of continual teaching, preaching, and celebration. Otherwise, the clericalizing tendencies of the ministerial elites will resurface again and again, as history shows.

Think, for example, of the complete rejection by the mid-nineteenth century papacy of the patient and carefully articulated efforts of European Catholic scholars to account for the compatibility of democratic reforms with Catholic tradition. Or take, as another example, the failure of the church's central administration to address and examine in detail the perspectives of the lay consultants to the papal birth control commission following the publication of *Humanae Vitae*. What might have been justly a prophetic moment for the church became instead a debacle that is bitterly remembered.

A current issue in the English-speaking world that is painful for many is the abandonment of inclusive language in liturgical texts. A coterie of powerful conservative bishops has managed to take control of liturgical translations into English in order to suppress inclusive language and any other liturgical expressions that suggest ecclesial decentralization or a stronger articulation of the particularities of the local church.

In all of these cases, the laity are the elements of the church most affected by the decisions of the leaders. Yet in these instances, as in many others, the views of the laity have not been taken into consideration. Until now, the laity have passively accepted the consequences of this unilateral use of authority in areas that are moot and practical. However, for a number of concerned and articulate Catholics, that day has passed. We can expect to see more examples like Voice of the Faithful and more exasperated defections from the Catholic community until meaningful lay consultation and participation become a greater part of parish and diocesan life.

Most twentieth century theologians have tried to correct the worst deformities of clericalism. The church itself has repositioned its own teaching. The Second Vatican Council created a framework for significant roles for the laity in church governance. In The Dogmatic Constitution on the Church, we read

> The sacred pastors . . . should recognize and promote the dignity and responsibility of the laity. . . . They should willingly use their prudent advice and confidently assign offices to them in the service of the church, leaving them freedom and scope for activity.[25]

As a result, many dioceses now employ laypersons in positions of great responsibility in church administration, such as diocesan chancellors, directors of the diocesan curia, and in various canonical and staff offices. In some places, however, these church-employed laypersons have become assimilated by extension into a wider clerical fraternity. Ironically, there is such a thing as lay clericalism. It seems to be contagious.

What has yet to be developed, in most cases, are structures that will engage the vision and energies of the laity out in the broader church. There are structures for synods, pastoral councils, and many varieties of parish committees. But at present the implementation of these structures, whether at the diocesan level or the parish level, depends upon the attitudes and interests of the administrator in question, whether bishop or pastor.

Nonetheless, the Code of Canon Law of 1983, the most recent formulation of official Catholic Church law, could not be clearer about providing a significant role for the laity in assisting the bishops in their governance. In Canon 212 §3 the following is legislated:

> [The faithful] have the right, indeed at times the duty, in keeping with their knowledge, competence, and position, to manifest to the sacred Pastors their views on matters which concern the good of the Church. They have the right also to make their views known to others of Christ's faithful but in doing so they must always respect the integrity of faith and morals and show due reverence to the Pastors and take into account both the common good and the dignity of individuals.

Much has been written and will continue to be written in an effort to interpret the challenge posed by the shock and public accountability related to the last few years of scandal. My responsibility here is not to interpret the social or ecclesial significance of the sex abuse scandals, but simply to point out how this event as a moment of destiny can be related to the topic of the priesthood of the faithful. I think that it is clear that a strong relationship does exist.

For too long we have loaded onto the roles of bishop and priest expectations of a heroic kind of exemplary holiness. Their roles have come to be so closely associated with the administration of the sacraments, and particularly with the consecration of the Eucharist, that people have come to consider them as "other Christs." We will see in due course that this is a meaningful phrase, but one which St. Paul assigns not to ordained ministers, but to all the baptized. Nothing in the pages that follow will call into question the need for bishops and priests or diminish their dignity. But what follows will put their ministry in a proper New Testament perspective. They are other Christs because they are baptized; they are servants of the Body of Christ because they are ordained. And most particularly, in their administration of Christ's sacraments, they are the symbol of Christ's headship in the midst of the Body of Christ as they lead the community in its rites of faith.

However, the true theological relationship of the ordained to the laity is not widely known or well understood. Bishops and priests themselves too often understand their role as utterly sacred personalities, beyond the reach of ordinary social understanding or accountability. As attorney Schiltz says, "One reason why a pastor could get away with abusing dozens of children in the past is that those who had evidence of such abuse—such as congregants or the victim's parents—simply could not believe that a pastor could commit such conduct. Needless to say, no one is laboring under that illusion today."[26] This crisis has been the occasion for a very public correction of the faulty notion that the ordained were beyond the reach of accountability. This was the hard way to learn the lesson. But it will prove to be an unforgettable lesson because of that.

Close to the end of his life, the great French theologian Yves Congar made an observation about his epochal book of 1953, *Lay People in the Church*. "I was criticized because I had defined the laity in terms of the clergy. Today it is the case, rather, that the clergy need to be defined in relation to the laity, who are quite simply members of the people of God animated by the Spirit."[27] For everyone's sake, it will be important for bishops and priests to internalize clearly that they are not a second "People" apart from the People of God. They could not be ordained if they had not been previously baptized. The most fundamental ecclesiological reality is the unity of the baptized in the one Body of Christ.

The baptized as the Body of Christ are the visible, earthly expression of Christ's heavenly priesthood and eternal ministry. So the priesthood of the baptized—meaning both the faithful and their pastors—has as its content the struggle for justice, the toil of love, the labor for community, and the compassionate ministry of mercy of all the faithful. These values become priestly precisely when they are joined to the paschal sacrifice of Christ in the celebration of the Eucharist. The church needs and will always need the ordained to lead the faithful in the celebration of gospel truth and the breaking of the bread. Such ordained ministers are drawn from the community of Christ's priestly people. Further, their ministry is a ministry of service ordered to the flourishing of the priestly life of the baptized.

So, it seems, we have ample warrant to explore the dimensions and dynamics of the priesthood of the baptized. In the next three chapters, we will pose these three questions: What do we mean by baptism? What then do we mean by Christian sacraments? And how do these ideas contribute to a proper understanding of the priesthood of Jesus Christ?

Notes

1. J.A.T. Robinson, *The Body,* Studies in Biblical Theology no. 5 (London: SCM Press, 1952).

2. Archbishop Sean O'Malley, "Why Preaching Must Be a Priority Today," *Origins* 33:45 (April 22, 2004) 722.

3. Bryan T. Froehle and Mary L. Gauthier, *Catholicism USA: A Portrait of the Catholic Church in the United States* (Maryknoll, NY: Orbis, 2000) 1f. [Hereafter cited as *CARA/Catholicism.*]

4. Ibid., 60.

5. This is a project of the Life Cycle Institute at Catholic University under the direction of Dean R. Hoge; their reports place the percentage of foreign-born priests at 16% or 17%. See Dean R. Hoge and Aniedi Okure, *International Priests* (Collegeville, MN: Liturgical Press, 2006 forthcoming).

6. *CARA / Catholicism,* 112.

7. William V. D'Antonio, James J. Davidson, Dean R. Hoge, and Katherine Meyer, *American Catholics: Gender, Generation, and Commitment* (Walnut Creek, CA: Altamira Press, 2001) 112. [Hereafter cited as *D'Antonio/American Catholics.*]

8. *CARA/Catholicism,* 154. See Philip J. Murnion and David DeLambo, *Parishes and Parish Ministers: A Study of Parish Lay Ministry* (New York: National Pastoral Life Center, 1999).

9. *CARA/Catholicism,* 151–5.

10. Ibid., 23. A recent Gallup Organization report shows that in December 2002, the percentage of Catholics who responded that they attended church "at least once a week" had declined to 28%. For the first time, Protestants (35%) are now more likely than Catholics to attend Sunday church services on a weekly basis. See "Catholic Church Attendance Drops This Year in Midst of Scandal" on the Gallup website at www.gallup.com. See "Catholics' Mass Attendance Continues Decline," *The CARA Report,* 9:1 (Summer 2003) 4.

11. *CARA/Catholicism,* 23.

12. Andrew Greeley, *The Catholic Revolution: New Wine, Old Wineskins, and the Impact of Vatican II* (Berkeley: University of California Press, 2003).

13. James D. Davidson, et al., *The Search for Common Ground: What Unites and Divides American Catholics* (Huntington, IN: Our Sunday Visitor, Inc., 1997) 189, 195 [hereafter cited as *Common Ground*]; see also *CARA/Catholicism,* 24–6.

14. *Common Ground,* 194–5.

15. Chögyam Trungpa, *Cutting Through Spiritual Materialism* (Boulder, CO: Shamabala, 1983).

16. *CARA/Catholicism,* 18. In 1990, 66% of U.S. adult Hispanics (9.5 million out of 14.5 million) were identified as Roman Catholics. By 2001, only 57% (13 million out of 23 million) were identified as Catholics. Cf. *The CARA Report* (Winter 2004) 4.

17. The website for the Association of Theological Schools provides information on students enrolled in seminary degree programs by denomination. See www.ats.edu (and click on Data). A highly renowned Hispanic Catholic leader told me that many Hispanics preparing for ministry in the U.S. Protestant

churches are not being trained in accredited seminaries, but in Bible Schools, and that the Protestant/Catholic Seminarian ratio is at least 5 Protestants to 1 Roman Catholic.

18. This ratio of three Protestant to one Catholic graduate student is verified in 2004 by the data of the Hispanic Theological Initiative at Princeton Seminary. An experienced Hispanic religious scholar wrote to me that "if you count the numbers in religious studies in secular universities, that ratio is probably more like 10 to 1. Hispanic Protestants already dominate the fields of church history, Bible, and religious studies in general. As a result they are the ones teaching our Hispanic Catholic students and providing them with a perspective on christian life."

19. Roberto O. González and Michael La Velle, *The Hispanic Catholic in the United States: A Socio-Cultural and Religious Profile* (New York: Northeast Catholic Pastoral Center for Hispanics, 1985) 144.

20. Nancy E. Bedford, "Little Moves Against Destructiveness: Theology and the Practice of Discernment," in Miroslav Volf and Dorothy Bass, eds., *Practicing Theology: Beliefs and Practices in Christian Life* (Grand Rapids, MI: Eerdmans, 2002) 176.

21. Robert McClory, "Bishops Ponder New Study of Priest Shortage" in *National Catholic Reporter*, 3 June 2000 (cited in *D'Antonio/American Catholics*, 102). Only 6.3 percent or 2,900 of the nation's 46,000 priests are Hispanic. Of these 2,900 Hispanic priests, approximately 500 were born in the U.S. Fifteen percent of the priests ordained in 2002 were Hispanic. There are 9,925 Hispanic Catholics per Hispanic priest, while there are only 1,230 Catholics per priest in the general Catholic population. Thirteen percent of current seminarians (about 500) are Hispanic. Only twenty-five (or 9 percent) of the nation's 281 active bishops are Hispanic. There is a ratio of one bishop for every 231,000 in the general U.S. Catholic population, but a ratio of one Hispanic bishop to every one million Hispanic Catholics. See data listed at www.usccb.org/hispanicaffairs/demo.html#4.

22. Patrick Schiltz, "Not All the News Is Fit to Print," *Commonweal* (Aug. 15, 2003) 14.

23. Ibid., 16.

24. Walter Conklin, "Interview with Jim Muller," *Notre Dame Magazine* (Winter 2002–2003) 29–31. For information about "Voice of the Faithful," go to <www.votf.org>.

25. Documents of Vatican II, Dogmatic Constitution on the Church, n. 37.

26. Schiltz, 15.

27. Bernard Lauret, ed., *Fifty Years of Catholic Theology: Conversations with Yves Congar* (Philadelphia: Fortress Press, 1988) 64–5.

Chapter 2

Chosen to Live

People sometimes have trouble tracking down their baptismal certificate when it comes time for their wedding, for entry into the seminary or religious life, or even for secular events that require an objective social record of birth date and identity. That was my case, years ago, when I applied to enter the Dominicans. Because of my mother's illness at the time of my birth and my own uncertain health as a newborn, I was baptized in the hospital and the records remained there, making them difficult to find. I mention this because I suspect that many people have had experiences like this in trying to track down the registry of their baptism. Even though Christians ought to believe that the day of their baptism is the most important day of their life, in fact, they most often come to take their baptism for granted.

A century ago, the American Baptist theologian Walter Rauschenberg complained that Christians' understanding of baptism had degenerated into a single self-serving idea—an "individualistic interpretation of [baptism] as an escape from damnation."[1] If people only want baptism to remove the curse of original sin and get that problem out of the way, then baptism might indeed seem to be only an event in the past with nothing much to do with the present. As with other bureaucratic records, such as birth certificates, titles to automobiles, and deeds to properties, our confidence that the record of our baptism exists is reassuring, but its bearing upon our day-to-day consciousness is vague or uncertain.

By contrast, if you are a serious Christian, then you never completely "dry off" from your baptism, to use a wonderful phrase of Gerard Baumbach.[2] The sacrament is a living reality, not merely an unrepeatable event in the past. The entire ritual of baptism, in fact, is designed in such a way as to be memorable. Those who were baptized as infants, as I was, will have no memories of their baptism, except perhaps by way of home videos or photographs. The impact of that moment is likely to be remembered by parents, godparents, and older siblings, especially if, instead of pouring water, the baby is immersed in the baptismal font.

For those baptized as adults at the end of a catechumenal process, the images of their baptism will long linger in their minds and imagination. One newly baptized adult remembered her baptism as "Getting water dumped on me! And this whole congregation looking at me . . . and I thought, 'O, my God' . . . and cheering . . . I remember everything . . . . it was so exciting."[3] Another newly baptized adult had this recollection: "All that was still new to me . . . symbols and all that stuff . . . I didn't understand them at the time . . . it was like, frightening . . . baptism . . . that was great . . . the big white robe you had to wear . . . it was gigantic!"[4] These might seem superficial observations, but they make it clear that the event was unforgettable for these two adult converts. And that fact is the seedbed for a lifelong harvest of graced meanings in the future.

For centuries, the Catholic Church has understood that the best way to lead people into an effective understanding of their baptism is through practical explanations of the Christian rites in the days following their baptism. In the early days of the church, the "enlightened" (the Greek name for the baptized) were offered weekly instructions called mystagogical catecheses—that is, instructions which initiated them into the mysteries that baptism had accomplished. The greatest example we have of these teachings is a series of twenty-four instructions that St. Cyril, bishop of Jerusalem, preached in the Basilica of the Holy Sepulcher around the year of A.D 350. His imagery is gripping and often dramatic.

"Water is at the origin of the world," he said; "the Jordan is at the origin of the Gospels; and baptism is at the origin of the Christian life."[5] For St. Cyril of Jerusalem, baptism is quite literally the beginning of a new life. He stressed that central theme over all else. By baptism, he insists, our lives are changed and we are given a new identity. The following lines that he preached in his cathedral in Jerusalem give us some sense of how momentous this change is meant to be for us:

Great indeed is the baptism you shall receive! It brings ransom for the captive, forgiveness of sins, death to sin, new birth for the soul. It is a garment of light, an indelible seal, a chariot bearing you to heaven. It is the delights of paradise, the gift of the kingdom, the grace of adoptive sonship. So prepare your heart for the reception of this teaching and for fellowship in the holy mysteries.[6]

Linger for a minute over this rich word *mystery*, because it is at the heart of what baptism should mean for us on a day-to-day basis. In current American popular usage the word *mystery* means little more than an unanswered question. In the New Testament, however, the word *mystery* refers to God's plan to reorient human history to a final destiny that is going to draw all creation into harmony with God. For example, think of this well-known passage: "With all wisdom and insight [God] has made known to us the *mystery* of his will according to his good pleasure that he set forth in Christ, as a plan for the fullness of time, to gather up all things in him, things in heaven and things on earth" (Eph 1:8-10). Here the Scriptures portray us as gathered up in God's transformation of creation when the destiny of the cosmos is revealed.

In the Greek theology of the Eastern churches, the word *mystery* means the same as "sacrament" in the Latin west. Both of these words are names for a holy sign that makes the invisible become visible, that brings God's eternal love into the present, and that is an instrument of communion between God and human beings. For example, Vatican II also uses the word *mystery* to mean the participation of baptized Christians in the life of Christ, because their participation in Christ's incarnation—the central mystery of the Son of God becoming human—is the means of the world's transformation. Accordingly, this theological idea of mystery most fundamentally means that God, who is impalpable and infinite, has chosen to become involved in finite and palpable ways in the fabric of our physical world. To the degree that we are instruments of God's involvement in creation as a function of our baptism, we are implicated in the mystery. What begins with the Son of God taking upon himself a human nature continues in humans receiving from the Incarnate Son the divine gifts of forgiveness, adoption, and the Holy Spirit.

In harmony with this perspective, the New Testament characterizes the mystery of baptism as having a multitude of meanings and exercising a variety of divine influences, a bit like Cyril's description above. Baptism is our purification, our new birth in water and the Holy Spirit, the replacement for circumcision, the seal of the Holy Spirit, and our illumination with the light of the risen Christ.

Furthermore, the effects of baptism make a person a temple of the Holy Spirit (1 Cor 6:19), a joint heir with Christ, and an adopted child of God (Rom 8). As a result of our baptism, the Father of Jesus has sent the Holy Spirit into our hearts to teach us how to act as God's children.

THE DIFFICULT CHALLENGE FOR PEOPLE TODAY

The daunting challenge for contemporary Christians, however, is to find a correlation between these exalted images and their own experience of life, which is so often overshadowed by meaninglessness. It is easier for those whose understanding of baptism is magical to jump ship. If they think baptism was supposed to snatch them out of the grinding toil of ordinary life and establish them firmly in spiritual security, then they are more likely to imagine the whole thing as a fairy tale.

The real story behind the mystery of baptism is the story of two worlds that coincide in Christ and in those who choose to become his disciples and to live in him. The world that is passing away and the world that is coming to be—the earthly and the heavenly—paradoxically coincide in the church and in each of the baptized. The paradox is that the dynamics of earth and heaven maintain their very different characteristics—one visible, the other invisible; one evident, the other hidden—despite their actual unification in the Christian life. What St. Paul promised to his Christian converts in Corinth is what he called "the first installment" of the gift of the Spirit (2 Cor 1:22; 5:5). The presence of the Holy Spirit of God in their lives would cleanse, heal, strengthen, and direct them through the choices and the duties of their lives, but it would not offer them an escape route from the hard toil and sufferings of ordinary life. The Spirit does indeed come and dwell with us, but we in turn are obliged to learn the language and the ways of the Spirit of Jesus.

So receiving the gift of the Holy Spirit does not dissolve the ambiguity of this hybrid new life as people who are being spiritually transformed. We continue to live in a world of "available reality," characterized by conflicts, uneven moral and relational development with those closest to us, competing visions and goals, and, of course, fatigue. In the midst of all this, our vocation as believers and disciples of Christ is to affirm our belief as a form of hope. Paul's letter to the Romans gives us this classic formula: "[S]uffering produces endurance, and endurance produces character, and character produces hope, and hope does not disappoint us, because God's love has been poured into our hearts by the Holy Spirit that has been given to us" (Rom 5:3-5).

We cannot afford to forget that sometimes the New Testament defines believers as those who still confess their unbelief: "Immediately the father of the child cried out, 'I believe; help my unbelief!'" (Mark 9:24). Is this not often true in our lives too? We set out trustingly in a friendship, a marriage, or a vocation, believing that God has guided us there. But all the contradictions and wounds of our past have come along with us on the journey. So before we arrive at the glory of a dream fulfilled, we have to face the crucifixion of confronting and converting our selfishness, our blindness to others, our fears, and even our resentment that life is not going to be easy. Any wide-awake adult, I believe, probably prays every day something like this prayer of the anxious father in Mark's Gospel: "Lord, I believe; help my unbelief!"

The late Russian Orthodox theologian, Alexander Schmemann, seized upon the simultaneous glory and irony of the predicament of faith when he wrote, "Baptism is . . . the only existential *proof* that Christ is risen indeed and communicates his risen life to those who believe in him."[7] The process of transformation that results from baptism alters lives so radically that they bear witness to the risen Christ into whom they are grafted. How else could we move on in our lives from what is deadly to what is life-giving, from what is selfish to what is gracious, from what is shadowed to what is luminous? The baptismal gift of the Spirit, which is the fruit of Christ's victory over death, enables us to shape our lives according to that mystery. Christ's rising is given to us now, to the degree that we are willing to take the path to true life through the dying process of purification and transformation.

OUR NEW IDENTITY

Our difficulty in bringing the ordinary stuff of life into contact with God's revelation and grace is not rooted exclusively in the poor match between our sloppy lives and God's divine perfection. Another major obstacle is that we do not really understand ourselves or our real destiny. As St. Augustine famously pointed out, our hearts are designed with a mammoth yearning that is not easily satisfied. Until we know what our lives are for, we will lack the fundamental tranquillity of a peaceful life. That infinite hunger, of course, is part of God's plan for us. It is the key that unlocks the door to real meaning and enduring life.

What are our lives intended to be? One of the essential ideas for understanding the effects of baptism is the theme of divine adoption. In Romans, Paul tells us that as believers we are "predestined to be conformed to the image of [God's] Son" (8:29). Earlier Paul tells us that "When we cry, 'Abba! Father!' it is that very Spirit bearing witness with our spirit that we are children of God, and if children, then heirs, heirs of God and joint heirs with Christ. . . ." (Rom 8:15-17)

What exactly, though, have we inherited with Christ? Why is this relationship with Jesus' *Abba* so important? As John's Gospel shows us, even the Twelve had difficulty grasping the importance of that. "Philip said to him, 'Lord, show us the Father, and we will be satisfied'" (14:8), and Jesus responded, "Believe me that I am in the Father and the Father is in me" (14:11). The short answer to the question "What have we inherited with Christ?" is that the only way to find out is to follow Jesus, to walk with him, and to be guided, as he was, by his Spirit. Jesus says to us what he said to the disciples of John the Baptist: "Come and see" (John 1:39).

The Gospels portray the disciples as those who were smitten with love for Jesus and fascinated by his preaching even though they understood very little of the mystery that he preached about the kingdom of God. Their attitude is summed up in Peter's words in John's Gospel. Jesus asks, "Do you also wish to go away?" Peter's reply is loaded with the ambivalence of genuine love and enduring perplexity: "Lord, to whom can we go? You have the words of eternal life" (John 6:67-68).

But the disciples not only have trouble understanding Jesus; they have trouble understanding what is going on inside themselves. The trouble with true self-knowledge is that it is not easily attained. Each person's life overlaps the boundaries of many others ranging over space and time. Many different people make claims on us, each with different expectations of who we are and what we mean for them. We do not really know exactly what is involved in fully becoming a person or where true fulfillment can be found. However, while that is so, we do recognize that we have received Christ's invitation to life. We have been grieved by the death of those near to us, saddened by the sickness and pain of our friends, fearful of our own vulnerabilities, and we know that our own death is a reality that looms somewhere on the horizon. Nonetheless we are still haunted by Jesus' claim: "I came that they may have life . . . ." (John 10:10) We want that life; the desire for it is part of what defines our humanity. To be human is to be hungry for meaning, for love, and for community.

LIVING THE MYSTERIES

Is there a method, a mechanism, a program, or a technique for getting at "life in abundance"? We will see that there is. But we will also see that it will require the sacrifice—the abandonment—of everything that we thought we understood about ourselves as well as everything that we thought we controlled in our lives. The method for receiving "life in abundance" includes unlearning our attachment to all the superficial cravings that are so aggressively vaunted by consumer culture. We need to refuse to allow ourselves to be defined by the commercial culture around us. There is no depth or stability—no real abundance of life—in consumerism.

Archbishop Kallistos Ware points out that there is a specific reason for the indefinable character of the human person: "It is because the human being is made in God's likeness, and since God is beyond understanding, his icon within humanity is likewise incomprehensible."[8] Ware further argues that this insight requires a "negative anthropology" to go along with our "negative theology." Negative theology is an approach in Christian theology that insists that all human language about God will necessarily be inadequate.

Because the Creator is revealed in creation, it is possible to say something about God using human categories such as "beauty, goodness, and power." But the reality of God transcends all such human concepts, and so the path to true knowledge of God is one of negation, pointing, as it were, to something about God, but acknowledging the incapacity of our ideas and language to reach the truth. A negative anthropology likewise would insist that whatever we are able to describe about our own humanity will be flawed and inadequate, and will require a way of negation. That is because the authentic meaning of our human existence can only be revealed to us in the mystery of Christ. Our vocation is to live our way into that authenticity, to follow the path of Christ as disciples.

The church teaches, moreover, that this is precisely what our Christian duty is. In its Constitution on the Sacred Liturgy, the Second Vatican Council speaks of baptism as a reorientation of life's meaning within a new context. In number 6, we read: "Thus by baptism men and women are implanted in the paschal mystery of Christ; they die with him, are buried with him, and rise with him. . . . They receive the spirit of adoption as sons and daughters . . . and thus become true adorers such as the Father seeks."[9]

The "paschal mystery" is the expression that Christian theology uses to name the process of transformation that baptized disciples experience on the path of following Christ. Our willing acquiescence in dying to distractions that can lure us away from the new life we have received in baptism is the living practice of a negative anthropology. There is suffering and sacrifice entailed in hard choices. However, disciples of Christ must choose continuously to live for the sake of the Body of Christ rather than for themselves alone, to express in their actions the self-giving love of their Master rather than the grasping self-interest of the "me-generation." In this way, through repeated struggles to make Christ "the Way" of their lives, the faithful set aside what is unprofitable and enter into an understanding of their new life.

A distinguished French Nobel laureate, François Jacob, has written a rich and interesting memoir describing how he made his way from humble beginnings to become an internationally renowned scientist. His book is entitled "The Statue Inside," and his narrative describes how, largely unknown to himself, through choices that were both thoughtful and instinctive, he affirmed some of his talents and potentialities and cast others aside.[10] Years of learning to see and feel deeply, of investing in the disciplines of a scholarly life and in friendships that spoke to his heart, led Jacob to create what he calls "the statue inside." In his maturity, he can look back and see how important certain moments, opportunities, and persons were for him. But now he *is* that inner statue, that moral construction of a disciplined, gifted, and generous human being.

François Jacob's story seems germane to me in this context. Like him, we have to learn the freedom to abandon everything but the image of Christ inside our complex, churning interior life. For us, as disciples of our Master, Christ himself is "the statue inside." We aim to configure ourselves to that model of a graced humanity.

The prayer of the church has always held out formulas that invite us to take part in this great mystery. For example, in one of the antiphons from Christmas, we read "Man's creator has become man, born of a virgin. We have been made sharers in the divinity of Christ, who humbled himself to share in our humanity." The Latin words that begin this ancient prayer, *"O, admirabile commercium,"* literally mean "What a marvelous bargain!" God offers us salvation and immortality if we are willing to offer to God our lives, our actions, and our passion for life. The cross of Jesus and his rising from the tomb are the foundation of this paschal mystery. Its essential theology is summarized in this familiar memorial acclamation from the Mass: "Dying, you destroyed our death; rising, you restored our life; Lord Jesus, come in glory!"

Suffering, loss, pain, grief, and death—everything that is worthless in the eyes of the world—become active instruments of God's power within the paschal mystery. Christ's triumph over death through his resurrection is our reason for hope in our moments of diminishment. "The logic of the paschal mystery is that the faithful, who are joined to Christ through baptism and the Holy Spirit, share in his passing over—passing through—human loss and suffering into a graced renewal of life. By following Christ through suffering and conflict in the hope of resurrection, his disciples are purified and transformed."[11]

Baptismal regeneration is not static, is not given in completeness once for all. Entering baptism is entering into a life-long dynamic state that requires constant attention and repeated adjustments. Each time a new insight is gained there are new implications for the mysteries of faith. Each time new social complexity enters our life, we must seek to understand its relationship to our fundamental vocation to follow Christ in the light of his mysteries. The choice of a profession, of a partner for life, of roles of leadership, and similar moments of decision ought to draw upon our identification with Christ and shape our future in ways that conform us more fully to his Spirit. In fact, any decision of ours that is influenced by Christ's example and power in our lives is an expression of the mystery of his incarnation shaping the contours of our spiritual growth.

The mysteries of Christ are not limited to what happened in the last week of his life. Many Catholics are familiar with the fifteen (now twenty) mysteries of the Rosary, each one of which describes a particular manner in which God entered human life through the incarnation of his son and through him achieved the salvation of the world. Each of these mysteries possesses a spiritual potency to illuminate the meaning of our lives, to guide us in understanding our experience, and to lead us through the events of our lives into our destiny as adopted children of God. In the prayer that concludes the Rosary, we say, "Grant, we beseech Thee, that meditating on these mysteries of the most holy Rosary, we may imitate what they contain and obtain what they promise. . . ."

That prayer expresses well the meaning of Christ's mysteries. They are a kind of blueprint for us. However, they do not provide us a formula for exact imitation of the precise actions of Jesus and his mother, but rather they provide us with examples of how we can integrate our life experiences into our relationship with God. They show concretely how the Spirit of God acted through Jesus' humanity to heal and reveal, teach and preach, and thus gather people into the Kingdom of God. There was no context that was off limits to Jesus' interaction with the people of his day. He entered completely into his social and cultural environment and changed the lives of those he encountered by his contact with them.

In a document called The Dogmatic Constitution on Divine Revelation, the Second Vatican Council uses an important expression that helps to clarify the meaning of Christ's mysteries for our Christian lives. In number 4 we read, "Everything to do with his presence and his manifestation of himself was involved in [his bringing revelation to its perfection]: his words and works, signs and miracles, but above all his death and glorious resurrection from the dead, and finally his sending of the Spirit of truth. He revealed that God was with us, to deliver us from the darkness of sin and death, and to raise us up to eternal life."[12] Every aspect of Jesus' earthly existence and physical presence was revelation. His saving incarnation reaches from the moment of his human conception to the moment of his resurrection.

French theologian Christian Duquoc developed this insight as the foundation for his christology, a rare work of contemporary theology that explores in depth the saving significance of the mysteries. He reminds us how clearly the New Testament affirms the transforming power of Christ's entry as Son of God into our humanity. The unfolding of Jesus' arduous preaching mission and his tragic encounter with death manifest countless points of engagement between our lives and his. Duquoc summarizes his point this way:

> To lead humanity to its fulfillment, the high priest himself experienced all the different stages of human life. The author of Hebrews is not thinking only of the passion of Christ: it is the entire life of the high priest which is in his mind. Hebrews goes out of its way to underline the truth of Christ's humanness: Christ has lived in a human condition like our own without reserve. The only difference between him and us is this: he is not a sinner (4:15).[13]

For centuries theologians have explored the significance of the events of the life of Christ, seeking to articulate the transforming power of Christ's incarnation through the course of his birth, growth, ministry, and passion, death, and resurrection. For example, St. Thomas Aquinas, writing in the thirteenth century, explored in depth the birth of Christ, the manifestation of the newborn Savior, his baptism by John, his manner of life, the temptation of Christ, his teachings, his miracles, and his transfiguration. These writings are contained above all in the third part of his *Summa Theologiae*, questions 27–45.

As a key to his interpretation of Christ's mysteries, Aquinas reminds us that the name *Jesus* means "Savior," and his saving works reveal his personal power and authority as Son of God. What Jesus does in his healing, exorcisms, preaching, and miracles is to show that the kingdom of God—the re-entry of the creator God into the framework of creation—has broken into the time and space of human history. As a result, time and space have become points of contact between this in-breaking kingdom and our own lives, when they are lived with faith in the power of Christ's mysteries.

THE ROLE OF THE HOLY SPIRIT

God helps us to make the needed connections. The sending of the Holy Spirit to believers is the gift of an inner movement—a comforting and reassuring touch—to lead us to both understand and accept divine truth beyond the reach of mere logic. In the explanation of the Vatican's special commission for the Great Jubilee, "Since the salvific actions of Christ were fulfilled twenty centuries ago, the 'task' of the Spirit has been that of making visibly present the resurrected Christ 'through signs,' so that Christ's salvific actions—his birth, life, teaching, miracles, and above all his death and resurrection—become 'contemporary' to people. The action capable of activating the 'mysteries' (salvific actions) of Christ in the church today is called the sacred liturgy."[14]

In every action of the church, we are called to a deeper faith and a clearer relationship with the entire Holy Trinity. The Trinity is the principal agent of Christian liturgy: "The Son made flesh is the living center of the liturgy, the Father is its origin and termination, but it is the Spirit who makes Christ present and contemporary in the Church."[15] All the mysteries of the life of Christ, along with all the actions of God in history from creation to the second coming, become real for the believer through the action of the Holy Spirit. The believer is led to the point of encounter between time and eternity through the Spirit's action. By invoking the Spirit (through a prayer which theologians call an *epiclesis*), the Spirit accomplishes a reactualization of the mystery of salvation. What Christ achieved for us then, becomes life for us now.

Baptism and the gift of the Spirit belong together. (A distinct sacrament, confirmation, bestows the personal gift of the Holy Spirit upon the baptized. Although the two sacraments are distinct, baptism and confirmation are complementary elements of a single initiation.) Through the gift of the Holy Spirit, a new internal principle deepens Christians' communion with the Father and the Son. The baptized are structured into one Body of Christ only because the same Spirit who anointed Christ also anoints all his members in their entirety. "Only then do these members become Christians. . . ."[16]

This anointing action of the Holy Spirit is what turns revelation from a story in the past to a possibility in the present. The opposite of what we might expect is in fact the case. We might imagine that our grafting into the Body of Christ presupposes the eradication of all conflict, struggle, and weakness in our lives. But this is not the case. Christ came not to find congenial companions, but to save sinners. His living Body, the church, is made up, not of sanctimonious persons who have removed themselves from the theater of human work and worry, but of everybody—the struggling and the serene, the earnest and the carefree, the generous and the stingy, the accomplished and the hopeless. Vigen Guroian, in a stimulating essay that wrestles with the intersection of grace and reality, cites this interesting passage from an essay of Flannery O'Connor:

> St. Cyril of Jerusalem, in instructing catechumens, wrote: "The dragon sits by the side of the road, watching those who pass. Beware lest he devour you. We go to the Father of souls, but it is necessary to pass by the dragon." No matter what form the dragon may take, it is of this mysterious passage past him, or into his jaws, that stories of any depth will always be concerned to tell.[17]

As Guroian says, no twentieth-century writer was more impressed than Flannery O'Connor with the Christian conviction that the Lord of all creation waged a successful battle against the powers of evil, and won. The often eerie quality of her writing is due precisely to her conviction that God really does touch actual persons and shape their lives, often in very strange ways. Likewise, she was sure, God chooses the poor and the ignorant as agents of his message as readily as he chooses the sophisticated and the well-educated. Reading Flannery O'Connor's stories is a solid antidote to escapist spirituality.

In consequence of Christ's victory over evil, his mysteries do not remain merely inspiring moral examples for us, but become transforming causes of our assimilation into Christ through our struggles with sin and evil. Christians who put their jobs and their professional lives on the line in order to stand up against injustice or corruption in the workplace are not just emotionally inspired by the story of the Gospel. They are moved by the grace of faith and the assistance of the Holy Spirit to dare to identify and confront evil.

We have not yet mentioned here (and will not study in depth) a very important part of the rites of baptism—namely, the exorcisms. These are powerful prayers addressed to Satan, the prince of darkness, and to the devils. In the name and the power of Christ, the minister of baptism commands Satan to depart from the one being baptized and to let go any hold that he has on the person's mind or heart.

Scripture tells us how the power of evil broke into human life and led our ancestors to sins of pride and idolatry. But then Christ came to reclaim human life from the demonic powers. Baptism includes a renunciation of Satan. In the rite of baptism, the one baptized is asked explicitly, "Do you reject Satan and all his empty promises?" This is another way of asking, "Do you reclaim your own human freedom in Christ for the sake of your new life?" "Do you refuse to let the powers of this world coopt your choices and your desires?" Genuine freedom is the fruit of a life delivered from the power of evil and compulsion.

REAL FREEDOM

Human freedom is the context for the power of evil to attack our human sensibilities. Satan will always try to entice us into thinking that God is cramping our style by putting unreasonable limits on our actions and personal expression. As in chapter 3 of Genesis, where the serpent (the symbol of evil) said to the woman, "Did God say, 'You shall not eat from any tree in the garden'?"; the power of evil today asks effectively, "Does religion/Christianity oblige you to give up every satisfaction, every individual choice, every moment of satisfying pleasure?" The strategy, of course, is to make the invisible Master of creation seem absurdly unfair, excessive in putting limits (like a natural law) upon intelligent beings like ourselves. Why would modern men and women who believe in their personal autonomy allow anyone (even God) to put a framework or restrictions on their self-expression?

It takes us a lifetime to learn that human freedom is not a reflex of reacting to others' initiatives. Above all, genuine freedom is not a state of wresting ourselves loose from the power of God. Freedom is a gift that God did not give to any other creature. God gave it to humans so that they could enter a graced relation of friendship with him. In Paul's letters, freedom is described as a God-given capacity to cooperate with God according to his plan of leading creation to harmony and glory. Human beings are, in a real sense, the conscience and the stewards of the material universe as a result of their participation in God's plan for the liberation and unification of all creation. This is the basis for the transforming influence of believers' faith on the world around them.

The self-determining freedom of the baptized is the freedom to claim in full all the prerogatives of those chosen to be children of God. "It is the graced capacity of a creature made in the image and likeness of God to become a son or daughter of God. Such sonship or daughterhood is not by nature but by grace."[18] Only grace can give us the freedom to pursue the most important friendship in our life, if that is friendship with God.

BENIGN CONTAGION

After talking as we have about the complexities of life and the obstacles to human freedom, we can return with deeper appreciation to the expression used in the early church as the name for the baptized—the "enlightened." What is the mystery that is the object of this enlightenment? The mystery of life itself is the object. Through faith in God's revelation, we have come to believe that we were created because of God's love for us. Our destiny is to live in friendship with God as our beloved, and our entire life can be invested with significance and generative power in the light of that relationship. The light of Christ shines on the whole of life for those who live in Christian faith.

Catholic moral theology places at the critical center of human responsibility the person's capacity to act intentionally. In simplest terms, this means to know what to do and to genuinely will to do it.

The positive benefit of living intentionally is that it gives you a powerful sense of direction. Lesser choices are linked to more important ones; ephemeral interests are evaluated in terms of lasting goals. In a theological perspective, our life is unified by organizing all of our piecemeal and passing decisions so that they serve the pursuit of one final, organizing option. For the Christian, that option is to live rather than to die, and to live with and in God.

Much of what we have been discussing under the topic of living our baptism as a life-long experience is the expression of this fundamental moral intentionality. Once you have found what the Gospels call "the pearl of great price," the one thing so good that you are willing to sell everything else you have to obtain it, your life changes. The clear intentionality of shaping every decision in life to make it coherent with the choice for God, brings clarity, energy, and peace. This is a rare phenomenon in our world today, I think. However, it is a potent quality that most often is attractive to others and influential in their lives.

A person who is genuinely free can be a powerful force. We've seen the Scriptures describe such a person as adopted by God, and also seen how St. Cyril describes this change as a new identity. A key question, I suppose, is this: "Do you have anyone in your life who offers you such illumination?" For millions of people around the world, the resolute determination of Mother Teresa of Calcutta to create hospices and centers for the dying and sick poor of the world was an inspiration and an example of an almost miraculous faith. Her freedom spilled out over countless lives to draw the abandoned into community and the despairing into environments of hope. A generation ago, Archbishop Oscar Romero gave reassurance and encouragement to the poor of El Salvador by standing up for them against a cynical and corrupt government. He gave his life as a martyr without fear, and his love for the poor changed their lives and their hearts, if not their destiny. People like these have a tremendous impact on the lives of others not only because of the achievements of their actions but also because of their witness to the power of the Holy Spirit to act through very ordinary human beings.

Sometimes the influence of a graced life is much simpler. A newly baptized woman spoke of her relationship with her husband in these words: "In him I see Christ, a lot . . . it's always 'calm down, take a deep breath, don't worry about it'!"[19] These are simple expressions of kindness and concern, but they obviously speak of an immense nurturing and reassurance that makes a life-giving difference in this woman's life. Another woman told me that Christ entered her marriage in a new way when she first saw her husband in an emergency room looking every bit as frail and battered as the crucified man on the wall behind him. His patience with chronic illness over many years became a sacrament of Christ's grace for her.

God's idea for the church is that it express in human gestures the proclamation of the kingdom of God and God's power to love, welcome, heal, and forgive. The members of the Body of Christ, through the power of the Holy Spirit, become a kind of benign contagion in society, gently spreading the vision and energies of Christ's Spirit through their human contacts. This outreach can happen in the simplest ways, as we have seen. What it takes is faith and the experience of living the challenges and hardships of life in the light of the mysteries of Christ.

Such human generativity, expressed in terms of the goodness and care of one human being for another, is really an expression of divine generativity. As we have seen, the work of the Holy Spirit makes such a transformed life possible. Baptism, the sacrament through which men and women are introduced to the life of the Spirit, allows them to live the mystery of Christ by living freely, as the people God intends for them to be. This is the foundation for living out the priesthood of the baptized. We will carry this understanding of the concrete expression of the Spirit's action in our lives, activating the mysteries of Christ, forward into the chapters that follow. The Spirit opens the door for us onto the grace of divine meaning in the midst of human darkness.

Is it possible that, after all this talk about the meaning of baptism, you feel too dry? Have you lost some of the dampness of your original baptismal grace? Fear not! You can be sure that the church will sprinkle you again on a regular basis. Catholic ritual never lets you forget the importance of your baptism. It is the sacrament that begins everything. But we need to know more about this idea of sacrament. What, after all, do sacraments do? That is the next step and what we turn to in the next chapter.

Notes

1. Walter Rauschenbusch, *A Theology for the Social Gospel* (Nashville, TN: Abingdon Press, 1978) 201, cited in Vigen Guroian, *Incarnate Love: Essays in Orthodox Ethics* (Notre Dame, IN: University of Notre Dame Press, 1989) 58.

2. Gerard F. Baumbach, *Experiencing Mystagogy: The Sacred Pause of Easter* (New York: Paulist Press, 1996) is a wonderful resource for establishing the life-long character of baptismal grace; he uses this imagery of "drying off" from your baptism on p. 1.

3. Ibid., 69.

4. Ibid., 74.

5. Cited in Guroian, op. cit., 55.

6. St. Cyril of Jerusalem, Procatechesis 16, in Lucien Deiss, *Springtime of the Liturgy* (Collegeville, MN: Liturgical Press, 1979) 274.

7. Alexander Schmemann, *Of Water and Spirit* (Crestwood, NY: St. Vladimir's Seminary Press, 1978) 112, cited in Guroian, 55.

8. "Foreword" in Panayiotis Nellas, *Deification in Christ: The Nature of the Human Person* (Crestwood, NY: St. Vladimir's Press, 1987) 9.

9. *Vatican Council II: Constitutions, Decrees, Declarations*, ed. Austin Flannery (Northport, NY: Costello Publishing Co., 1996) 120.

10. François Jacob, *La statue intérieur* (Paris: Editions Odile Jacob, 1987).

11. Paul Philibert, *Stewards of God's Mysteries* (Collegeville, MN: Liturgical Press, 2004) 3.

12. Vatican Council II, op. cit., 99.

13. Christian Duquoc, *Christologie: essai dogmatique*, vol. 1: *L'Homme Jésus* (Paris: Editions du Cerf, 1968) 212. See also vol. 2: *Le Messie* (Paris: Editions du Cerf, 1972). See also the rich treatment of the mysteries of Christ in the *Catechism of the Catholic Church*, Part One, Ch. 2, para. 3, n. 512–60.

14. *The Holy Spirit, Lord and Giver of Life*, prepared by the Theological-Historical Commission for the Great Jubilee of the Year 2000 (New York: Crossroad Herder, 1997) 91.

15. Ibid.

16. Jean Corbon, *The Wellspring of Worship*, trans. Matthew J. O'Connell (New York: Paulist Press, 1988) 113.

17. Flannery O'Connor, "The Fiction Writer and His Countryside," in *Mystery and Manners*, ed. Sally and Robert Fitzgerald (New York: Farrar, Straus & Giroux, 1969) 35, cited in Guroian, 58–9.

18. Guroian, 61.

19. Baumbach, 72.

Chapter 3

Living, Holy Signs

About ten years ago, I appeared as a guest speaker on a weekly program of TV station WLAE in New Orleans. The format was a fifteen-minute lecture presentation on the topic "What makes us Catholic?" followed by about fifteen minutes of responding to call-in questions from the audience. Naturally I mentioned the Catholic understanding of the sacraments in my lecture presentation. So it was not too surprising to receive a phone call from a woman who identified herself as Protestant and who asked this question: "In my church, we have only two sacraments; how come you Catholics have seven?"

Her question seemed a wonderful opportunity to clarify some very fundamental principles about Catholic belief, so I welcomed it. Briefly, I told her that before we talk about the seven sacraments, it is necessary to first understand that the most important Christian sacrament is the body of the Lord himself. Following that, the church itself must be understood as the sacrament of the risen Lord, and only then can we properly understand the meaning of the ritual actions which the church calls its sacraments. (Since this chapter is going to be about the very things that I was trying to explain to that caller, I will go no further in describing my reply to her question right here.)

At the end of the broadcast the station manager told me that this program was almost always carried weekly on a national cable network, but that the nun who ran that network had to approve the program. So he told me that next week I should be able to see a rerun on the network. However, two days later, he called to tell me that the nun who ran the network turned the program down with the comment, "Real Catholics only have seven sacraments, but that priest seems to have nine or ten."

It appears that this nun's criteria for what "real Catholics" believe do not include knowledge of the teachings of the Second Vatican Council. Since her thoughts on this may be representative of many Catholics, it may be worth our while to try to understand better the Christian tradition of sacraments, especially since our understanding of priesthood will be deeply affected by it. As we will see, the Christian people transformed by the sacraments are more important and strategic for the coming of God's kingdom than are the ritual actions themselves.

JESUS IS THE SIGN OF GOD WITH US

The words of the Scriptures are the best place to begin. In the New Testament, there are many indications that the disciples and the gospel writers understood Jesus as a living witness to God's action in their midst, a sign of God's presence, and thus Jesus himself was the fundamental sacrament or sign of God's action in the world. This is where we must begin. Two passages in particular (Matthew 12 and John 14) give us sayings of Jesus in which he portrays himself as a sign. Both of them are very instructive.

In Matthew 12, Jesus and his disciples are walking through fields of grain on the Sabbath day, and his hungry disciples begin to pick ears of grain and nibble on them. The Pharisees blame Jesus saying, "Look, your disciples are doing what is forbidden on the Sabbath." Presumably they mean harvesting grain. The scribes and Pharisees are portrayed here by Matthew as hardheaded and legalistic. As the rest of chapter 12 makes clear, in contrast to the Pharisees, Jesus places human needs over Sabbath observance. This becomes clearer through two healings which Jesus performs on the Sabbath in the sight of the scribes and Pharisees, one of a man with a withered hand (vv. 9-14), and the other of a possessed man who was both blind and mute (vv. 22-32).

By the time we get to Matthew 12:38, the antagonism between the scribes and Pharisees and Jesus is very strong. At this point, some of the scribes and Pharisees approach him with a request, "Teacher, we wish to see a sign from you." They are asking him for a miracle to prove that Jesus has divine authority. Jesus uses this exchange to foretell in veiled terms the real sign that will be the central message of his life: the resurrection. So he says to them, "An evil and adulterous generation asks for a sign, but no sign will be given to it except the sign of the prophet Jonah. For just as Jonah was three days and three nights in the belly of the sea monster, so for three days and three nights the Son of Man will be in the heart of the earth."

The sign that Jesus offered them is his victory over death. The Gospels plant the seeds of promise for Jesus' resurrection here, so that the mystery of Christ's new life might be understood later. The sign of Jonah means that the prophet is always in the hand of God, no matter what his apparent catastrophe. In the Old Testament book of Jonah, God lifted Jonah out of the impossible situation of becoming a sea monster's dinner. It is now clear in the light of contemporary biblical scholarship that the book of Jonah is a work of edifying fiction written long after historical Nineveh was destroyed in 612 B.C.E. However, it is also evident that this story was well known at the time of Jesus and was a narrative with strong symbolic meaning for the people of his day.

The parallel with Jesus is evident. The sign that Jesus is from God and acts in the power of God—exactly what the scribes and Pharisees asked him to prove to them—is that God pulls him out of the impossible situation (which we have all inherited) of physical death and corruption. Jesus is that unique sign from God of human flesh saved from the jaws of death by God's immortal power. He is the one—the one and only one—whom death cannot destroy. Our own immortality as baptized believers is dependent upon our being grafted as members into Christ's Body which has become immortal through his resurrection.

In the second passage, John 14, Jesus is found teaching the disciples as they linger at table on the evening of the Last Supper. He has shared with them that he is about to leave them to go to the Father. Jesus speaks with love and confidence of the care that his Father will have for his disciples. In this context, Philip asks, "Lord, show us the Father, and we will be satisfied." Jesus' reply to Philip is important for us: "Have I been with you all this time, Philip, and you still do not know me? Whoever has seen me has seen the Father" (John 14:8-9). This is an extremely important point for the evangelist John. Through this utterance of the Lord, John makes clear that Jesus is the definitive visible sign of God's special presence in this world. We can understand the power of Jesus' reply more fully if we look at some parallel passages in the same Gospel.

Remember the lines of John 1:18, "No one has ever seen God. It is God the only Son, who is close to the Father's heart, who has made him known." The message here is about Jesus' unprecedented relationship to God. This idea is put in even more dramatic terms in chapter 12 of John, "Whoever believes in me believes not in me but in him who sent me. And whoever sees me sees him who sent me" (12:44-45). John's Gospel here reveals to us that Jesus' message is no longer "words" from God like the message of the prophets, but rather the Word of the Father that remains the divine Word while becoming at the same time human being in human flesh.

God has poured out his divine power into a vessel that is earthly, vulnerable, and mortal—the body of Jesus. This great mystery of the Incarnation is not only a *kenosis* or "emptying out" of the Son (Phil 2:7), but an "emptying out" of the Father as well. The Greek word *kenosis* conveys the idea of setting aside prerogatives of power in order to reach into new areas of relationship and self-expression. In the Trinity, the Father completes his pouring out of himself into creation with this greatest gift of his creation, the birth of his Son in human flesh. As with every action of divine *kenosis*, the whole Trinity is at work at once.

The Father pours out his love upon the reality that he brings into being. As Father-Creator, God releases eternal divine energy into material being within space and time. The Son enters this created world to lift it up into a personal relationship with God. By living as God incarnate within our world, Christ the Son of God communicated to whatever he touched the characteristics of a potential bridge or link between heaven and earth. The Holy Spirit anoints these links or mediating symbols to render them sensitive to the divine action by actually dwelling inside the structures of creation. These are the actions, not of three gods, but of the one God whose life is expressed in mutual relations of generative love among three distinct persons. They share their mutual love in communion with us through the mystery of the Incarnation.

It took the Christian church more than four hundred years to adequately clarify its understanding of the mystery of Christ. In 325 the Council of Nicea (which gave us the Nicene Creed that we recite at Sunday Mass) rejected every teaching about Jesus that made him more than human but less than God. So in the Creed we pray "true God of true God . . . begotten, not made." The second General Council took place in 381 at Constantinople and insisted on Jesus' humanity against those who emphasized Jesus' divinity to the point of denying him a human soul. The Council of Ephesus in 431 continued the development of the church's teaching on Christ by clearly stating that the person Jesus is "true God" and therefore his mother is Mother of God. It was only in 451, at the Council of Chalcedon—the greatest of the first four General Councils of the church—that it expressed its profession of faith that Jesus Christ is:

> Perfect in his divinity and perfect in his humanity, true God and true man . . . , consubstantial with the Father by the divinity and consubstantial with us by the humanity, . . . generated by the Father before all ages according to the divinity, and in these latter days, for us men and for our salvation, by Mary, Virgin and mother of God, according to the humanity.[1]

Following Chalcedon, the enigmas generated by the divergent literary and theological traditions in the New Testament and addressed gradually in these first four General Councils are resolved in the profession of this common Catholic faith stated by the Council Fathers. All theology since has been an effort to resituate in a changing world the heritage of the apostolic age as expressed at Chalcedon. In this respect, these words of Pope John Paul II are suggestive: "[Christ] is God who comes in person to speak of himself to [us] and to show [us] the way by which to reach him. . . In Jesus Christ, the incarnate Word, time becomes a dimension of God, who in himself is eternal."[2] For our sake, the Son of God takes up a human nature, joining the divine and the human in a new life which is both pattern and possibility for those who become his disciples.

Christ accepted this new life of the Incarnation from his Father from whom he proceeds as Word, as well as from his mother, Mary, from whom he receives all the earthiness of our humanity. Two worlds come together in him. Jean Corbon speaks to this in moving language as he writes,

> [Jesus] was to be the meeting point of two loves and the focus of their covenant; the place where two piercing nostalgias met, but also the source of their satisfaction. . . . [In Jesus] God is born in a human being and a human being in God: a place of birth and connatural knowledge, a threshold which death is forbidden to cross, a silence filled with outpouring joy.[3]

The consequences of this central moment of human history are far-reaching. Because the Word "emptied himself" and came in the form of a servant—that is, in poverty and humility—those who followed him did not immediately understand the mystery that Jesus was. His *kenosis* meant choosing the path of poverty, of presence to the weak of this world, and of human vulnerability. This was a source of scandal, not only to the scribes and Pharisees, but to many others as well. Captivating in his presence and his power, Jesus still remained an enigma. To use the words of the Catechism, "From the swaddling clothes of his birth to the vinegar of his passion and the shroud of his resurrection, everything in Jesus' life was a sign of his mystery. . . . His humanity appeared as 'sacrament,' that is, the sign and instrument of his divinity and of the salvation he brings. . . ."[4]

Jesus' way of poverty elevates and integrates our human limitations into his sanctifying Incarnation. By taking our human condition upon himself, he shows us how it is possible for us to live a life of union with God in the midst of our earthly situation. By making our humanity the sign and instrument of his mission of healing and sanctification, he transforms the capacities of our physical condition. Our human poverty becomes not a barrier, but a bridge, and Christ is himself the way across that bridge into a new life.

Christ did not live his life for himself but for us; as we say in the creed, "for us . . . and for our salvation, he came down from heaven." Everything Jesus did had as its aim to raise human life to a new dignity. Because a sacrament is a sign that actually achieves what it signifies, Jesus has changed our humanity by his loving obedience to the Father. By becoming poor, Jesus enriches us by meeting us in our own poverty; by his submission to his parents in his hidden life, he transforms our obedience; by his preaching and teaching, his word purifies his hearers from ignorance and falsehood; by his healings and exorcisms, he took our infirmities upon himself.

The significance of Christ as sacrament is captured in these words of the Catechism: "In all of his life Jesus presents himself as our model. He is 'the perfect man,' who invites us to become his disciples and follow him."[5] Jesus is not only the revelation of the invisible God to our mortal eyes, he is also the revelation of a fully authentic humanity to us who have known only humanity wounded by sin. It is no surprise to say that life often does not make sense to us. It can only make sense in the framework of Jesus' revelation of what being human is all about.

The divine Son took human nature upon himself as a sort of "language" through which the saving actions of the Incarnation can be expressed. In that language of the Incarnation, he shows us that our human life is an instrument upon which God's Holy Spirit can play. The Holy Spirit manifests how Jesus is the sure sign of the time of our salvation, of the day of God's favor, by acting through his human presence and gestures. This is exactly what we read in Luke in the passage where Jesus says:

> The Spirit of the Lord is upon me, because he has anointed me
> to bring good news to the poor.
> He has sent me to proclaim release to the captives
> and recovery of sight to the blind, to let the oppressed go free,
> to proclaim the year of the Lord's favor. (Luke 4:18-19)

The Second Vatican Council warned that the church must always "safeguard . . . the transcendental dimension of the human person." It explained this by saying, "For humanity's horizons are not confined to the temporal order; living in human history [men and women] retain the fullness of their eternal calling."[6] Christ's solidarity with us in our human nature extends the scope of our destiny. The humanity of Jesus Christ has become God's alphabet, spelling out for our world our authentic fulfillment in eternal communion with God.

Theologian Daniel Bourgeois refers to Jesus as the

> personal pastor of all of humanity. His perfect human nature, which he received from Mary and all the actions that he performed through its expression became for everyone the sacrament of salvation. We have received complete salvation through this reality, and through it alone; just as through the reality of the resurrected humanity of Christ, those who receive salvation will "come . . . to maturity, to the measure of the full stature of Christ." (Eph 4:13)[7]

Christ as sacrament lifts our human condition into a state of dialogue with God and communicates victory over death for those who become united to him.

It should be clear, then, that the church's sacraments cannot be understood apart from the mystery of Christ himself as sacrament. Forty years ago, Dutch theologian Edward Schillebeeckx electrified Catholic theology with his book, *Christ the Sacrament of the Encounter with God*. He recaptured for the church the truth and the fruitfulness of understanding the humanity of Christ as the irreplaceable sacrament that makes saving friendship with God possible for us: "Once the Christian religion is seen as an encounter of God and man in Christ the 'primordial sacrament,' the sacraments in themselves [have to] be seen as inseparable from the whole economy of revelation. . . ."[8] That economy includes in a privileged way the reality which we call church. It too must be understood as a sacrament.

THE COUNCIL'S VISION OF CHURCH

The Second Vatican Council left no doubt about its understanding of the church. It's teaching was not about a church that *has* sacraments, but about a church that *is* a sacrament. In the opening paragraph of its Dogmatic Constitution on the Church, we read " . . . the church, in Christ, is a sacrament—a sign and instrument . . . of communion with God and of the unity of the entire human race. . . ." This is spelled out more fully in number 10: "[Christ] rising from the dead sent his life-giving Spirit upon his disciples and through the Spirit set up his body which is the church as the universal sacrament of salvation." In other words, the church is a living invitation to all human beings to experience unity with God both now and forever.

As we saw in the last chapter on baptism, the church is made up of the baptized who form one mystical person with Christ their head. As a sacrament, the church signifies the gathering together of the scattered children of God into a communion which unites them to one another and jointly to God. The Catechism notes that "Communion with the Holy Trinity and fraternal communion are inseparably the fruit of the Spirit in the [church's] liturgy."[9] From the letters of St. Paul, we know that the term *communion* is expressed equivalently in a variety of terms such as "configuration," "divinization," "participation," "assimilation," and "incorporation."[10] We are transformed, radically changed, by our communion with God through the Holy Spirit.

In the eyes of God the Father, the members of Christ's Mystical Body form one divinized reality with him. To be divinized means to be living in the Holy Spirit. The Catechism uses a striking image to express this: "The Holy Spirit is like the sap of the Father's vine which bears fruit on its branches."[11] This relationship between God's adopted sons and daughters and their head is the basis for the priesthood of the Body of Christ that we will be looking at in the next chapter. This new life introduces the baptized into a new frame of reference, expressed in a new language, creating a new atmosphere of possibility and hope. A configuration to Christ—as in Paul's vivid phrase, "For me, living is Christ" (Phil 1:21)—is brought about by this action of the Holy Spirit.

The action of the Holy Spirit makes them adopted children of God the Father (Eph 1:3-5). As Paul explains in Romans, when we receive the spirit of adoption, "It is that very Spirit bearing witness with our spirit that we are children of God, and . . . heirs of God and joint heirs with Christ—if, in fact, we suffer with him so that we may also be glorified with him" (8:16-17). These words of Paul are another reminder of the "marvelous bargain" God is giving us in the paschal mystery of Christ. We offer our lives in all their concreteness, and God offers us through the gift of the Spirit a share in the passage of Christ from dying to rising.

The central objective of all the ministry and worship of the church is to form and empower Christ's disciples who are God's adopted progeny. We have observed how patient Jesus was with his disciples as they failed to understand his teaching about his Father and remained fixated upon their own agendas for Jesus. As the church through the centuries is renewed with new members from new generations of be-lievers, this patient tutelage in faith remains an inescapable part of the church's activity. In time, believers come to understand the mystery of the great intimacy that God is offering them, and then they allow themselves to be touched at their depths by the Holy Spirit.

So far in this chapter, we have examined how the Gospels present their witness of Jesus as a sacrament or saving sign of his Father's presence, then how the documents of Vatican II and the Catechism affirmed the sacramental nature of the church. In the light of these important elements of theological background, we now turn to the church's seven sacraments and see how they are actions of the Risen Christ ministering to the church through the agency of the Holy Spirit.

THE SACRAMENTS: A SYNERGY BETWEEN MATTER AND THE HOLY SPIRIT

The Christian sacraments are the backbone of the church's liturgical actions. Sacramental celebrations call the parish together to become the visible living Body of Christ in a certain time and place. In every Christian celebration there is an outpouring of the Holy Spirit that

makes the mystery of Christ present to us. In every sacramental celebration, the presider begs the Father to send the Holy Spirit as Sanctifier. Theologians use a Greek word, *epiclesis*, to describe this specific
action which literally means an "invocation upon. . . ." It is a plea
for the Holy Spirit to act in our midst so that our material signs and
actions may be enlivened by God's power. A text of St. John Dama-
scene from the early eighth century offers a rich summary of the
doctrine:

> You ask how the bread becomes the body of Christ, and the wine
> . . . the blood of Christ. I shall tell you: the Holy Spirit comes
> upon them and accomplishes what surpasses every word . . . Let it
> be enough for you to understand that it is by the Holy Spirit, just
> as it was of the Holy Virgin and by the Holy Spirit that the Lord,
> through and in himself, took flesh.[12]

In every celebration of the sacraments, there is a prayer of invocation to call down the Holy Spirit—an *epiclesis*. In baptism, it is for the
Spirit to come into the water in which the catechumens are to be
baptized. "Here the Spirit really descends, enters into the water, and
transforms it into a divine milieu," writes Jean Corbon.[13] In the sacrament of reconciliation the outpouring of the Spirit is contained in the
words of absolution in which "Everything is 'loosed' because everything is set free by the communion that is the Spirit of the Lord. The
priest's prayer is a true *epiclesis* prayer."[14] As a living sign of Christ,
the Confessor intercedes with the Father through the Spirit so that
this Christian "who was dead" may "come back to life again."

In each celebration of the Eucharist, there are two such invoca-
tions of the Holy Spirit that are at the heart of the divine action of
the sacrament. In the name of the gathered assembly, the presider in-
vokes the Spirit to act so that their offerings of bread and wine may
become the Body and Blood of Christ (the first *epiclesis*). Then, after
the institution narrative, the presider prays that the Spirit may make
of those who eat this bread and wine "one body, one Spirit in Christ"
(the second *epiclesis*). Sent by the Father who hears the church's
prayer of invocation, the Spirit gives new life to those who celebrate
the sacraments of Christ. So, in their turn, Christians become sacramental realities—living signs of God alive in human flesh through the
synergy of the church's prayer and of the Spirit's anointing.

In this context, it is not an exaggeration to say that these two invoca-
tions bring about two *transubstantiations:* the first is the transformation

of bread and wine into the Body and Blood of Christ; and the second is the transformation of the believers into the Mystical Body of Christ. The difference is that in the second case the believers are already members of the Body of Christ, and the action of the Spirit makes them to be even more profoundly members of that body through the eating of the holy mysteries. "[Holy] Communion renews, strengthens, and deepens this incorporation into the Church, already achieved by Baptism."[15] Elsewhere, the Catechism adds: "Having become a member of the Church, [they] belong no longer to [themselves], but to him who died and rose for us" (cf. I Cor 6:19; 2 Cor 5:15).[16]

Experientially this means that the behavior of believers becomes so suffused with the action of the Spirit through faith and love that the paschal mystery of Christ becomes part of their frame of reference for more and more of what they spontaneously do and say. If we speak here of the body of believers as a sacrament of Christ living in the world, we are really talking about a people who have experienced the Spirit's outpouring in themselves. They ask for and receive the action of the Holy Spirit as the energy and the context for their day's work. Their daily prayer, prayer before meals, prayerful reading of the Scriptures, concerned prayers for their own needs and the needs of others are all moments of invocation that invite the release of the Spirit into the events of their day-to-day lives.

More than the isolated individual, it is the community above all that is the visible sacrament of Christ's presence. Because of the theology of the "Body" of Christ, the church has always placed a strong emphasis upon the corporate nature of spiritual transformation. In the light of this, we can see the great importance of the shared faith of the family, first of all, and then of the parish community. A family that believes and prays together is invoking the *epiclesis*, the outpouring of the Holy Spirit over their relationships and life together, even if they have never heard of this rather arcane Greek word. A parish that really nurtures and sustains genuine community through mutual service in education, service to the poor, political consciousness-raising, and shared prayer is invoking (in each of these ways) the outpouring of the Spirit on their parish life. In either instance, the family or the parish, the life of the Spirit is a force for cohesive unity that can overcome terrible challenges and pain as well as become the source for tremendous joy and fulfillment.

Eastern Orthodox theology places great emphasis upon this transformation, which they name "divinization," in Greek *theosis* (to make someone God-like). Orthodox theology expresses this mystery in terms of the gradual diffusion or penetration into ordinary life of the awareness and the power of the kingdom of heaven. Through the sacraments, especially the Eucharist, the faithful are transported into a new spiritual environment. This is the Orthodox Church's way of affirming that it is possible for ordinary Christians to begin to think of themselves and live out their lives in terms of "being in Christ" and "participating in divine life." So typical is this way of thinking for them that the liturgies of the Eastern Orthodox churches provide the substance of religious education and moral formation for their people precisely because this theme of divinization is so central to their worship.

For these Eastern churches, the sacraments are understood not as a discrete number of isolated actions through which particular sacramental graces are bestowed upon individuals by ordained ministers, but as aspects of the one great mystery that is the church. That mystery is nothing less than this: God sharing divine life with humanity, redeeming human beings from sin and death, and bringing them into the glory of immortality.[17] Through the sacraments, Christ acts upon those who are baptized into his Body by the agency of the Holy Spirit in order to transform them ever more deeply into living expressions of his life and mission.

THE EPICLESIS ECOLOGY

Because the role of the Holy Spirit pervades the sacramental life of the church, it is useful to think of the church in terms of an ecology of *epiclesis*. Current use of the word *ecology* often goes beyond its original context of the interdependence of living and nonliving elements in the natural environment. Here I am using it metaphorically to refer to a complex environment in which the interrelationship of the human and the divine produces life-giving synergies. We have already examined many ways in which the synergy of the invisible divine Spirit with the visible material world creates a graced sacramental effect. In that sense, speaking of an ecology of *epiclesis* means that the action of the Holy Spirit in a sacramental world provides genuine meaning for our Christian lives.

In an *epiclesis* ecology, graced sacramental action is ordered according to three stages of mutually interdependent development. The elements in question are these: symbolic matter, a graced sign, and a realized mystery. Let us take these one by one to see what they mean and explore their importance for our purposes. Understanding these elements will prepare us to see the characteristics of the different meanings of priesthood in the next chapter and help us understand the precise nature of the priesthood of the baptized.

In the church's sacramental life, the liturgy uses *symbolic matter* that by its very nature is already suggestive of energy and action. This is easy enough to see when we observe the use of water in baptism, oil in anointing, bread and wine in the Eucharist, and personal trust in the sacraments of reconciliation and in marriage. In each case, the matter in question already "means something." Some examples of the meaning of water include slaking thirst, giving life to plants, washing and cleansing, as well as the more threatening meanings suggesting chaos in nature associated with hurricanes, high tides, or floods. Whatever else comes to be added to the meaning of water as symbolic matter through the church's ritual words and action, those natural meanings will continue to be carried along as an essential part of the complex of the sacramental meaning. Put another way, the sacraments use symbolic matter precisely because of its natural potency to give meaning to ritual action.

In an *epiclesis* ecology, the invocation of the Holy Spirit upon the symbolic matter asks that all the natural dynamics that pertain to it be filled with the divine energy of God. In the case of water, we invoke the Spirit's presence to come upon the water and bestow it with power, which is now combined with the water's natural power. This makes the water into a *graced sign*. As such, it becomes the means to achieve the work that the church has been given to do: it transports someone through the waters of baptism from a life doomed to death into a new life destined for eternal fullness of life.

This same order applies in a parallel fashion to the other sacraments. For example, the invocation of the Spirit in Eucharist calls for the energy of God to transform humanly nourishing food into the Bread of Life. All the "natural" attributes of bread as symbolic matter—its readiness to be broken and shared, to satisfy hunger, to be a source of growth—are carried along into the new reality, which is the *graced sign* that we call the Body and Blood of Christ. Note that at this level of development the graced sign is clearly a *means*—a food to be eaten so as to transform those who eat in order to give them new life. The *end* is the unification of many members in one body in Christ; the *means* is the divine food they eat. As the effect of the Spirit's *epiclesis*, the Eucharist is a precious divine gift. That is why we call it in the liturgy "bread from heaven." But with equal clarity, we recognize its nature as a means to an even greater end, since the institution narrative itself gives us the Lord's words: "Take, eat; this is my body."

This *epiclesis* ecology is more clearly manifest in the case of the Eucharist than in some of the other sacraments. For, as we have already shown, there is a second invocation of the Spirit or *epiclesis* in the Eucharistic Prayer that asks that those "who eat this bread and wine, become one body, one spirit in Christ." This clarifies for us the third stage in the sacramental action, that of the *realized mystery*. Here we have no longer a means, as was the graced sign, but now an end. The realized mystery is the achievement and objective of Christian sacramental action. In each case, the church's sacraments lead to a "realized mystery," the creation or intensification of the mystery of the body of Christ. In the case of the Eucharist, this achievement is the transformation of those who eat the Body and Blood of Christ (the graced sign) into the Mystical Body of baptized members who find their life's meaning in the life of their head (the realized mystery).

In the next chapter we will look at how these ideas help us understand the relationship of the different aspects of Christian priesthood, one to another. For example, we will see how the ordained priesthood is a "graced sign" serving as a means to the end of the "realized mystery" that is the transformed life of the baptized in a living priesthood. But we are getting ahead of ourselves. That discussion belongs in the chapter that follows.

What is appropriate right now to this discussion of the dynamics of what I call the *epiclesis* ecology is some indication of the way in which the anointing of the Spirit animates and transforms the good works of every day. This teaching about the pervasive role of the Holy Spirit in the Christian life opens a window on the sanctification of our families, parishes, religious communities, and individual lives.

A structure similar to that which we saw in the church's sacraments is also at work in our Christian lives. The transformative dynamic of the paschal mystery depends upon the anointing of our actions by the Spirit. The same values are at work there as in the sacraments. What we called earlier "symbolic matter" can apply to the toil of our professional work, the struggles of our committed relationships, or any hardships in our lives whether coming from illness, disappointment, or betrayal. When we invoke the Holy Spirit to come upon these situations, they become a graced sign for ourselves, certainly, and potentially for others. The hardships of difficult but meaningful work—perhaps the leadership of parents in a family, executives in the workplace, or teachers in the classroom—become anointed and transformed with patience and love through the Spirit's gift. By grace, this will usually lead to some form of what we are calling the "realized mystery" of unity and harmony in the Body of Christ.

It is important for Christians to understand that this is God's plan for them. The in-breaking of the kingdom of God today can take many forms: angry people seeking a common ground in the midst of a dispute; couples with wounded feelings showing the humility to put their life-giving relationship ahead of defending their bruised egos; parents trying to teach their children to be self-sacrificing in a culture that values individualism and ambition; parish communities shaken by unforeseen conflict finding ways to return to important and unifying goals; and outraged citizens joining in solidarity to demand jobs for the unemployed or justice for the oppressed. You will have to name your own experiences of humility and honesty in the service of healing love; I can only evoke for you some of the typical contexts that are likely to be a part of anyone's life.

If you have experienced this grace of the Spirit's *epiclesis* upon the stuff of ordinary life, then you know the power that can emerge in such a moment. When the generosity of a married couple or the heroic patience of a teacher become "graced signs," they bring forth a disproportionate energy that goes beyond what the parties themselves are able to contribute. The unity that comes about as a result of such graced moments is often a deeper solidarity than what existed before the problem was manifest. That deeper solidarity is at the very least a participation in the "realized mystery" of a graced love in the Body of Christ, even if it remains less than perfect.

For anyone familiar with Christian theology, this will not seem too surprising. Jesus tells us in John's Gospel that he leaves us just one commandment, "Love one another as I have loved you." This commandment means not only love *just as much as* I have loved you, but also *in the very power of* Christ's love, participating in his love as a member of his body. Here we see both the source of the graced sign and of the effect of the realized mystery in the gift of the Spirit of Jesus who offers us the same love that is shared among the persons of the Holy Trinity.

As we draw toward the end of this reflection on the meaning of Christian sacraments, it will help if we make the transition between this discussion of the anointing by the Holy Spirit in the *epiclesis* ecology and the examination of priesthood which follows in the next chapter. The fundamental message behind this discussion of transformation by the Holy Spirit is that our capacity as families, parishes, religious communities, and individual believers to stand as living sacraments for the mystery of Christ's continuing incarnation comes from the Spirit's anointing which makes us into graced signs. We too are destined to become sacraments or signs of holiness in the midst of the church and of the world. To the degree that we receive the anointing of the Spirit, this transforming power that we have just described, we are both signs of that divine presence and instruments of its action in our world.

A text from St. Augustine can help us to get a clearer idea of spiritual anointing. In a commentary on Psalm 26, he wrote these powerful words:

> David was anointed king. In those days only a king and a priest were anointed. These two persons prefigured the one and only priest and king who was to come, Christ (the name "Christ" means "anointed"). Not only has our head been anointed but we, his body, have also been anointed . . . therefore anointing comes to all Christians, even though in Old Testament times it belonged only to [kings and priests]. Clearly we are the Body of Christ because we are all "anointed" and in him are "christs," that is, "anointed ones," as well as Christ himself, "the Anointed One." In a certain way, then, it thus happens that with head and body the whole Christ is formed.[18]

If we call believers "Christians" by virtue of their baptismal anointing by the Holy Spirit, so we also call all the baptized "priests" because, by virtue of that same anointing, they all are members of the only priesthood there is—the priesthood of Jesus Christ. What does this really mean? That is the topic for the following chapter.

Notes

1. Denziger-Schönmetzer, *Enchiridion Symbolorum*, §301.
2. *Tertio Millennio Adveniente:* Apostolic Letter of John Paul II in preparation for the Jubilee of the Year 2000 (1994) §6, 10.
3. Jean Corbon, *The Wellspring of Worship*, trans. Matthew J. O'Connell (New York: Paulist Press, 1988) 24.
4. *The Catechism of the Catholic Church* [hereafter *Catechism*], n. 515.
5. Ibid., n. 520.
6. Vatican II, *Constitution on the Church in the Modern World*, n. 76.
7. Daniel Bourgeois, *La pastorale de l'église, Manuel de théologie catholique*, vol. xi (Luxembourg: Éditions Saint-Paul, 2000) 133.
8. Cornelius Ernst, "Introduction," in Edward Schillebeeckx, *Christ the Sacrament of the Encounter with God* (New York: Sheed & Ward, 1963) xvi.
9. *Catechism*, n. 1108.
10. See *Jesus Christ, Word of the Father, Official Catechetical Text in Preparation for the Holy Year 2000* (New York: Crossroad-Herder, 1997) 124. [Hereafter, *Jesus Word of the Father.*]
11. *Catechism*, n. 1108.
12. Cited in *Catechism*, n. 1106.
13. Corbon, op. cit., 112.
14. Ibid., 115.
15. *Catechism*, n. 1396. For the idea of two transubstantiations as described here see Hans Urs von Balthasar, *The Glory of the Lord: a Theological Aesthetics, vol. I Seeing the Form*, 570–5.
16. Ibid., n. 1269.
17. John Meyendorff, *Byzantine Theology: Historical Trends and Doctrinal Themes*, 2nd edition (New York: Fordham University Press, 1983) 191.
18. St. Augustine, *Ennarationes in Ps. XXVI*, II, 2; cited in *Christifideles Laici*, post-synodal apostolic exhortation of John Paul II on the vocation and mission of the laity (Dec. 30, 1988), ¶14.

Chapter 4

A Priesthood
Embracing Christ's Body

On October 11, 1962, one of the most momentous occasions in recent church history took place in Rome. A little after 9:00 in the morning, the procession for the opening Mass of the first session of the Second Vatican Council made its way down the aisle of St. Peter's Basilica. Pope John XXIII had managed, in his words, to "open some windows" in the Vatican to let in fresh air, and his ecumenical council would inaugurate a new era for the church. A number of witnesses wrote down their impressions of that opening liturgy. Their remarks can give us a context for understanding the idea of priesthood that eventually emerged out of the work of the Council.

One of the most detailed accounts of the Council can be found in the diaries and reflection articles of the French Dominican theologian Father (later Cardinal) Yves Congar. Congar had suffered persecution and even exile under the papacy of Pope Pius XII. He was accused of being a major player in the Priest Worker Movement in France after World War II (he was not), and along with several others he was forbidden to teach or live in Paris for many years. The Vatican, which in the 1940s and 50s was very critical of his progressive theological ideas, used the crisis over the priest workers in 1954 as a cover to humiliate Congar and diminish his influence. By 1962, however, Congar had been "rehabilitated" by Pope John XXIII's personal invitation to become a member of the Council's preparatory commission. In the short span of a decade, he had moved from being regarded as a dangerous and troublesome thinker by the papacy of Pius XII, to being regarded as a creative and esteemed theological expert by the papacy of John XXIII.

Even though he suffered serious medical problems and was still deeply suspect in the eyes of the conservative Vatican establishment, Congar threw himself into the back-breaking work of preparing materials for the bishops and the Theological Commission. He wrote briefing papers, composed drafts, and mended diplomatic fences, especially with the Protestant observers and the Orthodox representatives whom John XXIII had invited to be present at the Council. Congar's extraordinary efforts left him almost constantly exhausted, but he gladly gave himself, hoping against hope that this Council would transform a church which he considered complacent and insensitive in ecumenism and inattentive in its pastoral practice among the poor.

The Council was an event of international scope. On television, via TeleStar, the whole world watched an opulent display of Renaissance grandeur calculated to feast the eyes and ears with brilliant color and lavish sonority. The world also watched an aging Pontiff bless the crowds from a chair mounted on poles, called a *sedia gestatoria*—a mobile throne carried on the shoulders of richly liveried valets. The Pope was periodically moved to tears by the emotion of the moment. They saw, in short, a production devised by the Vatican old guard whose aim was to trump the pretensions of any earthly power and (surely) to give ostentatious witness to their faith in God's providential presence within the institution of the Roman Catholic Church. It was glorious.

What Congar saw was different. He viewed the opening day of Vatican II through eyes that for years had recognized the narrow horizons of Roman bureaucracy, and he experienced the moment with a heart that yearned for freedom and openness to the rich variety of cultures in the world church. It is instructive, therefore, to consider his reactions to the opening ceremonies. The following lines are taken from his diaries of the Council for October 11, 1962:

> At 8:35 a.m., we begin to hear the distant sound of a sort of military march. Then they sing the *Credo*. I came here to pray: to pray *with*, to pray *in* [the Church]. And in fact I have prayed a lot. However, to kill the time while waiting for Mass to begin, the choir sang in succession anything and everything: the *Credo*, the *Magnificat, Adoro Te, Salve Regina, Veni Sancte Spiritus, Inviolata, Benedictus.* We tried to sing along with them a bit, but then gave up trying. . . .
> [Somewhat later] we heard applause in St. Peter's Square. The Pope must be coming—and entering. I can't see a thing, since there are some six or seven rows of young clerics in cassocks standing

on the chairs in front of me. Now [the procession is] inside the basilica: moments of applause—but no cries or words. . . .
Mass begins, sung exclusively by the Sistine Choir: some pieces of Gregorian chant (?) and some polyphony. The Liturgical Movement has not made it as far as the Roman Curia. This immense assembly neither says anything nor sings anything.[1]

The "liturgical movement" mentioned here refers to various initiatives in Europe and North America especially to reform the church's sacraments and public prayer so as to engage the faithful as active participants (rather than spectators) and to link their family and social life to their faith and worship. This movement had been a force in grassroots Catholic renewal efforts for more than a century.

Congar was not the only one to find the opening Mass deeply disappointing. The widely influential German liturgist, Joseph Jungmann, was also there, and he felt much the same. He later described the opening Mass as:

A High Mass without distribution of communion. Instead of integrating the opening actions (gospel in several languages, address of the pope, profession of faith, intercessions . . .), all these gave the impression of being an appendage without any order. . . . Perhaps the idea was to make clear the *terminus a quo* [what we have to leave behind] in matters liturgical![2]

Congar remarked that on the following day he was invited to a reception at the French Embassy where he met the Lutheran theologian Oscar Cullmann who was one of the most renowned Scripture scholars and ecumenists among the European Protestant observers at the Council. In discussing the opening Mass, Cullmann remarked: "So is *that* what your liturgical movement looks like?"[3] Congar, as the leading Catholic ecumenist in Europe at the time, found this understandable criticism mortifying.

As he sometimes did, Congar inserted a brief prayer in the midst of his account of that opening day: "Dear God, you have led me here by ways I would never have chosen for myself. I offer myself to you, if you want that, to be an instrument of your Gospel in this event in the life of the Church—a Church that I love but wish were less 'Renaissance'! less Constantinian."[4]

This last remark—an insider's expression among theologians— refers to the baptism of the Emperor Constantine by Pope Sylvester in the middle of the fourth century. The emperor's submission to the pope established Christianity as the "official" religion of the Roman Empire. This turn of events had led to an attitude of lordly condescension toward the secular world on the part of popes throughout most of Western history, an attitude that Congar considered far from dead in Rome.

Less than two weeks later, Congar met with a French bishop, Leon Elchinger, to discuss the Council's draft document on the liturgy. "I asked him to make an intervention [in the council hall] in the discussion *De Liturgia* [On the Liturgy], in order to request that the document clarify that the theological basis for the laity's participation in the liturgy is their priesthood. We put together a brief statement along these lines."[5] It was this theological concern that motivated Congar's interest in the conciliar liturgies and what they were implicitly teaching (albeit unknowingly) with their clerical and hierarchical liturgical style.

REDISCOVERING BAPTISMAL PRIESTHOOD

Congar was reacting to an entrenched clerical attitude that understood priesthood as the exclusive preserve of the ordained. His whole life's work had aimed at the retrieval of the theology of the priesthood of all the faithful as proclaimed in the Scriptures and understood through the early centuries of Christian theology. Watching the spectacle of the Council's opening liturgy implicitly proclaim a narrow clericalism through its style of celebration was understandably painful for him.

The Mass does not belong to the ordained. Public worship is the liturgy of the Mystical Body of Jesus Christ, head, and members. More important, perhaps, the rites of the church's public liturgies are not the only mission of the church. These liturgies are the visible (symbolic) expression of a Spirit-driven life whose mission is cosmic in scope. It is not bishops and priests who bring the ferment of the paschal mystery into daily contact with the work of the world; it is the faithful. Christ came to save the world, not to improve Temple worship.

Largely as a result of Congar's previous scholarship and his ceaseless assistance to the commissions of the Council, council documents emphasize the theology of the priesthood of the Body of Christ at several critical points. Rooted in the priesthood of the faithful, certain key texts serve as wellsprings of theological reflection about the Council's teaching on the church and the Christian life. It will be good for us to examine some of these conciliar statements in this regard.

The Constitution on the Sacred Liturgy, known in its official Latin text as *Sacrosanctum Concilium* (SC), was the first document of the Council to be completed, voted on, and published. In significant ways, it set the agenda for the Council. Even though its focus was liturgy, its vision of the church was so strong that its principles shaped the development of many of the later documents. Here are some of the dominant principles of this document:

> SC 7: The liturgy . . . is an exercise of the priestly office of Jesus Christ. In the liturgy the sanctification of women and men is given an expression in symbols perceptible by the senses and is carried out in ways appropriate to each of them. In it, complete and definitive public worship is performed by the mystical body of Jesus Christ, that is, by the head and his members.[6]

This important early statement of the Council clearly establishes that the whole Body of Christ—all the baptized—bring Christ's priestly action to earth. The Dogmatic Constitution on the Church, a later document of the Council, expresses the same idea in saying, "Taking part in the Eucharist sacrifice . . . [the baptized] offer the divine victim to God and themselves along with him" (n. 11). This text is describing the aspect of Eucharist that we called "the realized mystery" in the previous chapter.

For centuries, the faithful had been dispossessed of their proper role in the Eucharist, thinking that the Mass was the action of the ordained which they piously watched from afar and from which spiritual benefits trickled down to them. They did not fully own what St. Augustine called "their own mystery" of their unity with Christ their head. How did this state of affairs come to be?

For centuries the clergy were literate and the faithful illiterate. The ordained were also set so far apart from the rest of the faithful by their vesture and ritual gestures that the people felt themselves to be in another world from their liturgical leaders. For centuries, the Christian sacraments in the West were celebrated in Latin, a foreign tongue not understood by the vast majority of the faithful. In addition, the power of the clergy in controlling access to the church's liturgical rites became a bargaining chip in disputes over church life or policy. By the use of excommunication or interdict, the ordained created the impression that the world of sacraments was their world, and that others entered only at their bidding. And they excluded the faithful from the sacraments until they complied with the will of the bishop or the pope when they judged that force was needed, a practice in place to this day.

For that reason it is of the highest importance that The Constitution on the Sacred Liturgy establishes the principle that in every Christian liturgy, the primary celebrant is Christ himself. Through the Spirit's action, Christ who is at the right hand of the Father makes his divine liturgy present to us here in our assemblies. Christ is present to us as the one who acts to sanctify in all of the sacraments "so that when anybody baptizes it is really Christ himself who baptizes" (SC n. 7). He is present in his word proclaimed, present in the assembly, present when the church prays and sings, because he promised "where two or three are gathered in my name, I am there among them" (Matt 18:20).

Christ always includes the members of his body, the Church, within his priesthood's great work to glorify God and sanctify believers. Our present liturgies, in our own time and place, are the corporate action of a priestly people who, because of their baptism, now act together with their divine Master. So they share in "that heavenly liturgy which is celebrated in the holy city of Jerusalem toward which we journey as pilgrims, where Christ is sitting at the right hand of God, minister of the sanctuary and of the true tabernacle" (SC n. 8).

The Constitution on the Sacred Liturgy also contains one of the most beautiful expressions of this theology of the solidarity of Christ and his church in n. 83:

> Jesus Christ, high priest of the new and eternal covenant, taking human nature, introduced into this earthly exile that hymn which is sung throughout all ages in the realms above. He joins the entire community of humankind to himself, associating it with himself in singing his divine song of praise. For it is through his Church itself that he continues this priestly work. The church, by celebrating the Eucharist and in other ways, especially the celebration of the divine office, is ceaselessly engaged in praising the Lord and interceding for the salvation of the entire world.

This image of the church's life of prayer is fundamental to the theology of The Constitution on the Sacred Liturgy. The idea of a hymn brought here to earth by Christ through the Spirit's action reminds us that authentic liturgical acts are rooted in God's initiative. God invites, God speaks, God acts, and God sends. Although hidden from our eyes, this song of Jesus Christ is a gift that introduces our lives to the mystery of eternal life. The liturgy invites us to discover the eternal significance of our lives inserted into the mystery of God's incarnation.

The "hymn" of Christ is a metaphorical expression here. Christ's divine song of praise is in fact his humanity expressing itself as God's idea of Spirit and flesh was meant to be expressed. Christ's "song" is ultimately identical with his Incarnation. The Lord's humanity sings out God's divinity.

In chapter 3 we observed how Christ's presence and action is a kind of epiphany in each moment of his life. His whole life manifests what it looks like for divine Spirit to be poured out upon human flesh. The Constitution on Divine Revelation (n. 6) expressed this idea in these words: "[Jesus Christ] completed and perfected revelation and confirmed it with divine guarantees. Everything to do with his presence and his manifestation of himself was involved in achieving this. . . ." Christ's solidarity with us in our human condition is also the path for our entering the mysteries of Christ, as we showed in the second chapter.

In the liturgy, believers surrender in faith and obedience to the gift of God's Word and to the movement of the Holy Spirit. We are invited to become "one body, one Spirit in Christ" and to sing a great Amen to God's offer to allow us to live "through him, with him, and in him." The rites of the church presuppose that we do more than just listen and observe; they presuppose that we give ourselves fully and unguardedly to this divine work of transformation.

We saw above how the second *epiclesis* of the Mass prays that those who eat Christ's Body and drink Christ's Blood may become a new creation in the Holy Spirit. This is the transposition of the hymn of Christ into the gathered community. The realized mystery of the Eucharist is meant to become a real, present, and historical song that knows grief and joy, fear and hope, failure and survival, doubt and intrepid faith. The musical notes will be different from place to place; the language will be distinct for the great variety of communities of faith, and the rhythms will vary. But, if God's work is rightly done, this hymn of Christ will be sung throughout the church by people transformed by the Spirit.[7] That is why this text (SC n. 83) identifies the faithful's life of prayer as their exercise of priesthood.

PRIESTHOOD IN THE ORDINARY

Following upon the publication of the Constitution on the Sacred Liturgy, the theology of the laity and their role in the life of the church remained a central concern for the Council's leading figures.[8] It would require a long and dramatic story to describe fully how the Council's Dogmatic Constitution on the Church (in Latin, *Lumen Gentium*—LG) made its way from an initial draft that maintained the ecclesiology of First Vatican Council to the final version. Suffice it to say that the theological perspectives evolved considerably. *Lumen Gentium* begins with a first chapter entitled "The Mystery of the Church," and second chapter on "The People of God." Only after these two chapters does it introduce its consideration of the church's hierarchy. LG does not center itself on the prerogatives of the hierarchy, as did Vatican I, but on the solidarity of all the baptized with their Lord in the Spirit.

The freshness and theological focus of Vatican II's Constitution on the Church flows consistently out of the vision of its Constitution on the Sacred Liturgy. When *Lumen Gentium* describes the vocation of the laity, the text reads as follows:

> They live in the world, in each and every one of the world's occupations and callings and in the ordinary circumstances of social and family life which . . . form the context of their existence. There they are called by God to contribute to the sanctification of the world from within, like leaven, in the spirit of the Gospel, by fulfilling their own particular duties. (LG n. 31)

This presence of the faithful in the world is linked to their participation in Christ's priesthood in which "The baptized, by regeneration and the anointing of the holy Spirit, are consecrated as a spiritual house and a holy priesthood, that through all their Christian activities they may offer spiritual sacrifices and proclaim the marvels of him who has called them out of darkness. . . ." (LG n. 10). This phrase "spiritual sacrifices" refers to all our human actions anointed by the grace of the Holy Spirit and performed with the intention of pleasing God.

How can this inspiring and exalted theological imagery be connected to our own experienced reality? How can this call to sanctify social reality become a convincing, prophetic challenge to healthy, ordinary people in the world? It is one thing to express an edifying wish for people to be religiously serious, but it is quite another to convince them that their lives are organically implicated in God's most important plan for the world. Where is the bridge between these realities so distinct in the mind of most believers?

One of the most important testaments to the Christian vocation in contemporary theology is *Lumen Gentium* n. 34. This text focuses the Council's theological vision for the faithful, linking human experience explicitly to the priesthood of Christ in terms of what I like to call "priesthood in the ordinary," in which it reads:

> To [the laity], whom he intimately joins to his life and mission, [Christ] also gives a share in his priestly office of offering spiritual worship for the glory of the Father and the salvation of humanity. Hence the laity, dedicated as they are to Christ and anointed by the Holy Spirit, are marvelously called and prepared so that ever richer fruits of the Spirit may be produced in them. For all their works, if accomplished in the Spirit, become spiritual sacrifices acceptable to God through Jesus Christ: their prayers and apostolic undertakings, family and married life, daily work, relaxation of mind and body, even the hardships of life if patiently borne (see I Pet 2:5). In the celebration of the Eucharist, these are offered to the Father in all piety along with the body of the Lord. And so, worshiping everywhere by their holy actions, the laity consecrate the world itself to God.

This paragraph makes explicit the idea that the normal daily activities of the faithful, "if accomplished in the Spirit," are eucharistic. The attention is given here not to the rite or to the sacramental elements of bread and wine, but to the assembly gathered in faith to offer their lives. The actions of the faithful who are re-membered in the Body of Christ by the "realized mystery" of the Eucharist become a dynamic force for the sanctification of society.

A PEOPLE SANCTIFIED AND SANCTIFYING

How may the ordinary life and actions of the faithful be seen as an expression of the mystery of the Eucharist? In the previous chapter, we described an ecology of *epiclesis*. We drew a parallel between the Spirit's action in the church's sacraments and the sanctifying action of the Holy Spirit in the Christian. For a quick review, remember that the structure of the church's sacraments involves three interrelated stages beginning with "symbolic matter," moving toward a "graced sign," and aiming at "realized mystery." Let us relate this to the

Council's text on the priesthood of the faithful. As we just saw, the faithful's "prayers, apostolic undertakings, family and married life, daily work, relaxation of mind and body, hardships of life" are the symbolic matter of their "consecration of the world to God" (LG n. 34). The outpouring of the Holy Spirit acts upon this "symbolic matter" and makes it a "graced sign."

In daily Christian living as in the liturgy of the Eucharist, the "realized mystery" is a sanctified people who have become "one body, one Spirit in Christ." This sanctified people in turn become a *sanctifying* people. It is here we find the link between the priesthood of the faithful and their apostolic effervescence. The Dogmatic Constitution on the Church incorporates the faithful into the mission of the church and identifies their critical importance for its success. "The laity . . . are given this special vocation: to make the church present and fruitful in those places and circumstances where it is only through them that it can become the salt of the earth" (LG n. 33). The frontiers of the church's mission are the actions of the faithful as witnesses to their eucharistic life.

The development of this teaching helps to clarify the meaning of the priesthood of the faithful. "They live in the world, in each and every one of the world's occupations and callings and in the ordinary circumstances of social and family life. . . ." This phrase is a key to the theology of "priesthood in the ordinary." It is another way of saying that the Christian life is a comprehensive integration of human experience into what some theologians have called the "ongoing incarnation"—bearing in mind the need to respect the absolute uniqueness of the incarnation of the eternal word in Christ.[9]

Here is a clear parallel between Christ and the Christian. The Gospels go out of their way, as we have already shown, to describe the preaching and ministry of Christ as the outpouring of the Holy Spirit upon Christ's humanity. Christ's missionary activity, along with every other aspect of his redemptive incarnation, is an integral part of his priesthood. And now we see that the priesthood of the baptized, in a way similar to Christ's priesthood, is the offering of our humanity and our human actions anointed in the Holy Spirit. By the Spirit's anointing, human generosity becomes transformed into incarnational grace.

The faithful's presence and activity in the world are not only sociological phenomena, but theological realities as well. As we have seen, all the actions of Christ's incarnation, including his hiddenness and his silence, are integral to his revelation of God to humanity. Likewise all the actions of the members of Christ's mystical body have a potential to reveal the presence of the Risen One and the power of his Spirit set loose in the world. By seeking the kingdom of God in their temporal affairs and ordering them to the purposes of the Gospel, all these activities become part of God's plan of salvation.

This theological theme was close to the heart of Pope John Paul II. He used a powerful image to evoke the significance of the Council's theology of the priesthood of the laity in his apostolic exhortation entitled *The Lay Members of Christ's Faithful People*:

> The eyes of faith behold a wonderful scene: that of a countless number of lay people, both women and men, busy at work in their daily life and activity, oftentimes far from view and quite unacclaimed by the world, unknown to the world's great personages but nonetheless looked upon in love by the Father, untiring laborers who work in the Lord's vineyard. Confident and steadfast through the power of God's grace, these are the humble yet great builders of the kingdom of God in history.[10]

To describe this apostolic dynamic of the faithful as an expression of their priesthood makes even clearer the meaning of "spiritual sacrifices" offered to God as "graced signs" oriented to the "realized mystery" of Christ's transformation of the human world.

UNDERSTANDING CHRISTIAN PASSOVER

I have no doubt that some of my readers will find themselves scratching their heads with bewilderment at this point. After examining the Council's clear teaching of how the priesthood of the baptized finds expression in "spiritual sacrifices" that are part of the stuff of ordinary life they will be asking, "But the sacrifice of the Mass is the sacrifice of Calvary, isn't it? Is not Christ's self-sacrifice unique and redemptive precisely because he is both God and man?" How can we understand how Christ's gift of himself and our gift of our lives fit together?

First of all, it should be clear from what we have already said that the only sanctifying quality or theological significance of the "spiritual sacrifices" of the baptized comes from their being united to the sacrifice of Christ. The action of the Holy Spirit in the sacrifice of the Mass incorporates the lives of the Christian assembly into the new creation of the Body of Christ. Christ's Body is both the social-historical body of the faithful, and the unique, divine reality of God's eternal Word in human flesh. We call this the "Mystical" Body of Christ because it remains a mystery beyond the powers of our logic to penetrate and because it demands that we understand it in terms of our future destiny in a new life after death. The "not yet" of Christ's eventual triumph over sin is made present in the "already" of the church in witness and worship.

As for understanding Christ's sacrifice, there are various ways in which the Scriptures show us the meaning of that. Several threads are woven together here to help us grasp the mystery of Christ's redemptive incarnation. As the liturgy of the church always does, when we celebrate the Lord's dying and rising, we constantly refer to God's saving actions throughout human history. The liturgy finds images and prefigurings of Christ's saving deeds in the story of God's people in the Old Testament. Christ is understood to be the fulfillment of all the promises that God made throughout the ages of biblical faith. This same dynamic of promise and fulfillment also continues into our Christian lives, where the promise of Christ's death and resurrection is fulfilled through our living participation in his paschal mystery.

One of the liturgy's favorite expressions of Christ's paschal mystery comes from Paul's letter to the Philippians. In the hymn to Christ in chapter 2, we read that Jesus "became obedient unto death, even death on a cross" (Phil 2:8). Jesus is the second Adam who came to restore a humanity wounded by the sin of the first Adam (cf. Rom 5:12). Philippians sees Jesus' suffering and death, not as a punishment for Adam's sin, taken on himself for our sake to placate a disappointed, bitter, or angry God. Rather, Jesus' paschal journey is the forging of a pathway back to God and to Paradise at the initiative of the Father, a pathway closed off by Adam's rebellion. "Therefore God also highly exalted him . . ." (Phil 2:9). This is the mercy, and not the wrath, of God. So, we are exhorted to "let the same mind be in you that was in Christ Jesus" (2:5)—i.e., the spirit of *kenosis*, humility, and obedience to God's rule over our lives.

Another thread for understanding the sacrifice of Jesus is to perceive how Jesus transforms suffering into an instrument of salvation. Suffering and death will inevitably be part of the experience of every human being. Every one of us will know experiences of cruelty, injustice, disappointment, loss of those we love, confusion, and fear. The church interprets Christ's incarnation as his entering into solidarity with all these dimensions of our human fragility and suffering. Christ gives them a new value through the grace of his presence and the healing power of his love. To become a disciple, to agree to "Come, follow me" as Jesus asks, includes finding our way in faith through these vulnerable areas of our experience.

We remember these powerful words of Jesus: "If any want to become my followers, let them deny themselves and take up their cross daily and follow me. For those who want to save their life will lose it, and those who lose their life for my sake will save it" (Luke 9:23-24). It is not suffering as such that is the source of our redemption, but rather suffering as a sign of love—"for my sake." The paschal mystery of Jesus reveals to us both the profound disorder of our human condition and the power of suffering, accepted in love as a disciple of Jesus, to overcome evil. Jesus makes it clear that in the eyes of God it is not human force or the power of success that counts for anything, but rather the force of love which both heals and unites. We lose our life for his sake out of love. This is the only meaningful sacrifice that a Christian can make.

The letter to the Hebrews interprets Jesus' paschal mystery in the light of his innocent suffering. Hebrews sees Jesus' death and resurrection as the fulfillment of the promise given by the prophet Isaiah of a redemptive "suffering servant" who is beloved in the eyes of God (Isa 52–53):

> In the day of his flesh, Jesus offered up prayers and supplications, with loud cries and tears, to the one who was able to save him from death, and he was heard because of his reverent submission. Although he was a Son, he learned obedience through what he suffered; and having been made perfect, he became the source of eternal salvation for all who obey him. (Heb 5:7-9)

When we spoke above in chapter 2 of the "emptying out" of Jesus, his *kenosis*, we said that this was a *kenosis* of the Father as well. In all God's actions toward humanity, the whole Trinity is mutually engaged—and this is true above all of the Paschal mystery. The cross is not the story of a human Jesus paying the price for humanity's sin because his unyielding Father demands full punishment for the fault of Adam and Eve, and only Jesus (who is both man and God) can pay the price. That would be a caricature of divine revelation, even though, sadly, it is often what people think is the case. Neither is the sacrifice of the Mass primarily an activity of human beings directed to God, hoping to receive the reward of blessing and forgiveness in response to our earnest religious efforts. Both of these are misconceptions.

Rather, the Christian understanding of sacrifice starts with the self-offering of the Father in the gift of his Son to humanity—this is the Father's *kenosis* or emptying out (cf. "For God so loved the world that he gave his only Son, so that everyone who believes in him may not perish but may have eternal life" John 3:16). The sacrifice of Jesus Christ is the unique response of the divine Son in his humanity to the initiative of his Father, made in obedient love. Although the Son's sacrifice finds its culmination in the three days of his dying, burial, and rising from the dead, it integrates every aspect of his redemptive incarnation from his conception to his resurrection. This Christian Passover has become the passageway for humanity back to God through following Christ in his suffering, death, and rising to eternal life.

The sacrifice of Christians is their own self-offering in union with Christ, by which their very lives become the material for the offering of the church in its eucharistic presence in the world. Robert Daly explains that Christian sacrifice is not a God-directed action of human beings, but an event that begins with the initiative of God the Father. It is not just an "initiative" of the Father, but the "self-offering" of the Father in the gift of his Son "whose 'response,' in turn, is also a self-offering."[11] As Daly puts it, "In plain terms, sacrifice is not something that the Father does to the Son; and thus, since all authentic sacrifice begins here, authentic sacrifice can never be something that someone does to someone else. At its core, sacrifice is *self*-offering/ *self*-gift—in the Father, and in the Son, and in us."[12]

To go back to the problem posed earlier, how can Christ's gift of himself and our gift of our lives fit together? We affirm that the suffering of Jesus is unique in its essence (the passion of the God-Man) and in its consequences (the restoration of communion between God and humanity). But we can also now clearly affirm the complementary role of the "spiritual sacrifices" of Christ's members. For they show that the victory of Christ over sin and death is not an extrinsic event that changes our spiritual destiny from the outside, as it were, but a true intrinsic renewal of humanity. By entering and negotiating our human condition, Christ has turned it into a pathway to immortality. He has become, as he promised, "the way, the truth, and the life" (John 14:6). His death and resurrection opens up for us a participation in God's life of divine communion through our integration by baptism into the Body of Christ.

THREE ASPECTS OF THE ONE CHRISTIAN PRIESTHOOD

Before concluding this reflection on the priesthood of the whole Body of Christ, we need to make explicit what is already implicit in the reflections we have done so far. It is now clear that there are three meanings of the priesthood of Christ. The first is Christ's own ministry of mediation between God and humans. He is, as the letter to the Hebrews describes him, "the high priest according to the order of Melchizedek," "holy, blameless, undefiled," who "by a single offering . . . has perfected for all time those who are sanctified," that is, by his unique sacrifice of the cross. In the words of St. Thomas Aquinas, "Only Christ is the true priest, the others being only his members."[13]

The Catechism, in its account of and development of the teaching of Vatican II, carefully clarifies two other meanings of Christian priesthood. In number 1546, it says "The whole community of believers is, as such, priestly. The faithful exercise their baptismal priesthood through their participation, each according to his [sic] own vocation, in Christ's mission as priest, prophet, and king. Through the sacraments of Baptism and Confirmation the faithful are 'consecrated to be . . . a holy priesthood.'"

We have explored this priesthood of the faithful at length, expressed in terms of what the Council, borrowing from 1 Pet 2:5, calls "spiritual sacrifices." In the coming chapters we will explore further how this priesthood of the faithful is expressed in terms of each of the qualities of Christ's priestly mission—as priest, prophet, and king— just noted in the text of the Catechism above.

The Catechism goes on in number 1547 to describe the third meaning of Christian priesthood:

> The ministerial or hierarchical priesthood of bishops and priests, and the common priesthood of all the faithful participate, each in its own proper way, in the one priesthood of Christ. While being ordered one to another, they differ essentially. In what sense? While the common priesthood of the faithful is exercised by the unfolding of baptismal grace—a life of faith, hope, and charity, a life according to the Spirit—the ministerial priesthood is at the service of the common priesthood. It is directed at the unfolding of the baptismal grace of all Christians.

In chapter 3, we pointed out that the church itself is a sacrament to the world. It is a sign of humanity's communion with God and a sign of the communion of human groups with one another. Because

Christ is our principle of reconciliation, our mediator with God and the source of unity of all peoples, the Church ceaselessly celebrates in a sacramental way Christ's action among us.

We also noted in the last chapter the structure of Christian sacramental life, building upon "symbolic matter," receiving from the Holy Spirit "graced signs," and leading to the "realized mystery" of Christ's socially embodied presence. In this chapter we have pointed out particularly how the holy actions of the faithful can become spiritual sacrifices in solidarity with Christ.

As we conclude this reflection on priesthood, we should also note the clear link between the ministerial priesthood of the ordained and the "graced sign" of Christian sacramental life. The Catechism describes the ministerial priesthood as at the service of the priesthood of the faithful and directed to the unfolding of the baptismal grace of the faithful. This ministerial priesthood has its own sacrament, called the sacrament of Holy Orders. Holy Orders bestows upon the ordained a unique configuration to Christ to allow them to serve in the midst of the community of believers as a symbol of Christ as head of his body assembled in faith.

Only these ordained members of the body receive the power of invoking the Holy Spirit in the Eucharist and in some other sacraments (confirmation, penance, anointing, and holy orders). The sacramental quality of the ordained, then, makes them a sign of Christ's initiative in sanctifying his church. Here Christ as author and agent of salvation is sacramentally signified through them as the means of salvation for his disciples. This service of Christian priesthood as the means of the church's sanctification is directly linked to the aspect of sacrament called the "graced sign." The ordained, presiding over the assembly of faith, nourish them in word and sacrament so that the assembly will themselves become a living expression of the Body of Christ in the world. Likewise, the ordained lead the faithful as a sign of Christ's headship in their mission as prophets and pastoral leaders as well.

This also helps us to understand more clearly the priesthood of the baptized. In terms of their sign value in the church, the faithful are not seen under the aspect of "graced sign," but rather under the aspect of "realized mystery." They are the achievement, completion, and fulfillment of the church's sacramental life. It is the assembly that is the new creation, the royal priesthood, the people of God. Their transformed life and transforming actions are the goal of the Christian sacramental order.

For the moment, then, we can conclude this present reflection on priesthood with the affirmation that these two forms of participation in the priesthood of Christ—that of the faithful (a group in which, of course, the ordained remain a part) and that of the ordained—express the full reality of Christ which the church is obliged to manifest in history. This analysis provides a basis to understand the evident necessity of the ministerial priesthood as a work of loving service, on the one hand, and the superior dignity of the common priesthood of the baptized, on the other. As the Catechism makes abundantly clear, the ministerial priesthood is entirely relative to and finds its fulfillment in the cultivation of the baptismal priesthood.

The church as a sacrament, which is a sign and instrument of salvation, needs nothing more than this. Its entire sacramental reality is constructed upon the interaction of these two priesthoods which are the living expression of Christ's heavenly ministry for the transformation of the world.[14]

Notes

1. Yves Congar, *Mon Journal du Concile*, vol. 1 (my translation) (Paris: Éditions du Cerf, 2002) 106–7.

2. Andrea Riccardi, "The Tumultuous Opening Days of the Council," ch. 1, in Giuseppe Alberigo and Joseph Komonchak, eds., *History of Vatican II*, vol. II (Maryknoll, NY: Orbis, 1997) 12. It is interesting to reflect on the observation of Hans Urs von Balthasar, unconnected to this conciliar liturgy but relevant to its analysis: "Mass without communion (something impossible for the celebrant as representative of the community) is impossible and meaningless for the Church as such. . . ." Hans Urs von Balthasar, *The Glory of the Lord: A Theological Aesthetics, vol. I: Seeing the Form* (San Francisco: Ignatius Press, 1982) 574.

3. Congar, op. cit., 112.

4. Ibid., 107.

5. Ibid., 143.

6. *Sacrosanctum Concilium*, n. 7.

7. Cf. Paul J. Philibert, "Is There Still a *Canticum Perenne*? Where Can It Be Found?" *Worship* 74:3 (May 2000) 223f—a more extended reflection on SC n. 83.

8. Several chapters of Alberigo and Komonchak, *History of Vatican II*, vol. II, describe the background meetings and discussions that created the transition between the liturgy constitution and the work on revelation and church.

9. This was an idea frequently expressed by the Dominican theologian M.-D. Chenu, who was an influential expert among the European bishops at the Council. See Christophe F. Potworowski, *Contemplation and Incarnation: The Theology of Marie-Dominique Chenu* (Montreal: McGill-Queen's University Press, 2001).

10. John Paul II, *Christifideles Laici* (The Lay Members of Christ's Faithful People), post-synodal apostolic exhortation on the vocation and mission of the laity (Dec. 30, 1988) n. 17.

11. Robert J. Daly, "Sacrifice Unveiled or Sacrifice Revisited: Trinitarian and Liturgical Perspectives," *Theological Studies* 64:1(March 2003)24–42; here 27–28.

12. Ibid., 28.

13. *The Catechism of the Catholic Church*, n. 1545, cites this phrase of Aquinas' commentary on Hebrews.

14. The development of the theology of this chapter owes a large debt to the writings of French theologian Father Daniel Bourgeois. See for this ch. particularly D. Bourgeois, *L'un et l'autre sacerdoce* (Paris: Desclée, 1991) 177–80.

Chapter 5

People Who Speak for the Spirit

In this chapter we are beginning to explore how the priesthood of the faithful, which we described theologically in chapters 1 to 4, is shaped and expressed in terms of the three "missions" or tasks of prophecy, pastoral concern, and liturgy or worship.

In this and in the following two chapters, we will first examine the manifestation of this trilogy in Christ and then, by participation, in the members of his body. Beginning with this chapter, we will explore the significance of the prophetic charism of baptismal priesthood. In the next two chapters, we will look at the royal and priestly charisms. The final chapter will explore how the Christian doctrine of the priesthood of the faithful calls for response in the church today.

Let us take a very brief look at the history of the terms *prophet, king,* and *priest* through Scripture and church history. We will see that, for the ancient Christian world, these three titles were central to people's thinking about both Christ and about the faithful who are baptized into Christ.

In the Old Testament, all three of these roles—prophet, king, and priest—were intermediaries between God and the people of God in different ways. The prophet was anointed or called to teach and explain God's wisdom, the king to guide and defend the people according to God's covenant promises, and the priest to mediate in offering the sacrifices of the people before God. Many of the New Testament texts that we have already examined in earlier chapters take these Old Testament roles and their significance for granted—e.g., the letter to the Hebrews, the First Letter of Peter, or the book of Revelation. Jesus is seen in them as the fulfillment of everything that was promised in the Old Testament in the figures of prophet, king, and priest.

There is good evidence that the use of this threefold attribution in the church's theology is very old. For example, a fourth century document *The Apostolic Tradition*, contains this trilogy of roles in a text for the bishop's blessing of oil. The bishop prays that God will sanctify the oil so that it will become a source of holiness for those who use it and receive it: "With [oil] you anointed kings and priests and prophets."[1] The context suggests that this is a familiar theological idea for the time. Early Christian writers (e.g., Jerome, Gregory of Nyssa, and Augustine) also use these three titles in speaking of Christ. These and other authors in the early centuries take these titles for granted as names attributed to Christ by the Scriptures.

During the Middle Ages, however, the importance of the prophetic, royal, and priestly offices of Christ and of the faithful fell into the background. Early medieval controversies over how the bread and wine could become the Body and Blood of Christ led theologians to emphasize the unique powers of the ordained to consecrate, with the result that *ordained* priests became in the people's mind the *only* priests in the church. At the time of the Reformation, however, John Calvin revived interest in these three offices of Christ and made them the framework for his theology of Christ as Savior in his *Institutes of the Christian Religion.*[2]

In the twentieth century, the trilogy of prophet, king, and priest was prominently included in several major documents of Vatican II, in large part due to the influence of Yves Congar. In an important article on this topic published in 1983, Congar remarks "In Christ first of all, then also in the Church, there is a close mutual interrelationship of these three elements that goes like this: the functioning of one mission affects those of the other two. Royalty is both priestly and prophetic; prophecy is both priestly and royal; and the priesthood is both prophetic and royal. This is likewise true among the people of God."[3] It will be well for us to keep this close interrelationship of these missions in mind as we go along.

The council's fundamental objective in putting emphasis upon the three missions is to show the complementarity and equal dignity of the roles of teacher, leader, and sanctifier in the life of the church. The trilogy in the council documents sought to clarify the scriptural foundation for a priesthood of the faithful in the Constitution on the Liturgy, to examine the prophetic vocation of the faithful in the chapter on the Laity of the Constitution on the Church, and to explain how the ordained presbyter offers a ministry that is more than cultic, in the Decree on Priestly Life and Ministry. Put rather simply, preaching is as important as—maybe more important than—presiding at Mass in the light of this theology. The Great Commission of the Lord that concludes the Gospels of Matthew and Mark is "Go, preach!"

A clear choice of the council was to use the triad of prophet, king, and priest to increase awareness of the Third Person of the Holy Trinity. We have said enough in previous chapters to make the case for the very strong theology of the Holy Spirit at work in the teaching of the council. From a biblical perspective, prophets, kings, and priests were all ministers whose integrity depended on their capacity to open themselves to the movement of God's Spirit. During the high prophetic period of Israel, prophecies, particularly in the prophecy of Isaiah, became increasingly explicit about the gift of the "Spirit of the Lord," that is, the illumination and insight that came upon the prophet as a result of the Spirit's anointing or visitation. In Luke 4, Jesus refers back to this Spirit theology in Isaiah as the legitimation of his ministry in Galilee: "The Spirit of the Lord is upon me, because he has anointed me. . . ." (Luke 4:18).

We discussed in chapter 3 the role of the Holy Spirit as the dynamic principle in the life of the church. What the Spirit touches is transformed. The role of the Holy Spirit in the church's teaching, leadership, and sanctifying is both clarified and emphasized through the use of this analysis. The Spirit is everywhere at work in the church's prophecy, pastoral concern, and cultic action.

Based on this understanding of the work of the Spirit, Vatican II's explanation of the nature of the church is essentially missionary. It is the Spirit who prompts Christians to offer an evangelizing witness to the world. This is precisely why the three missions of Christ pertain to all of the members of his body, not just to the ordained. The opening words of the Constitution on the Church are "Christ is the Light of the nations." The church's fundamental mission is not the administration of ecclesiastical institutions and the celebration of sacraments *by* the hierarchy *for* the faithful. Rather it is the proclamation of the kingdom of God in both word and action by the whole people of God for the whole of humanity and the whole of the cosmos.

We can look again at Congar's insight into this trilogy of roles—prophet, king, and priest—with fuller understanding now. The *prophetic* will always have both a pastoral and a cultic dimension. That is, the church's teaching at whatever level will be effective when it is characterized by a loving concern for those whom it addresses and when it leads them to thanksgiving and praise. Likewise the *pastoral* will always have both a cultic and a prophetic dimension—understanding its care for people as complete only when it leads to a restored relationship with God in the community of faith, and when it offers a real understanding of human experience in the light of divine revelation. And finally the *cultic* or *priestly* will always have both a pastoral and a prophetic dimension in which it addresses the Christian assembly with sensitive awareness of their specific gifts and needs, and offering a true mystagogy (explaining the mystery of Christ) that opens up the liturgy to contemplative communion with God.

This close interrelationship of all three elements, one with another, reinforces the fundamental understanding of the life of the church as missionary. It is easier to see how essential prophecy, pastoral concern, and worship are when each is placed within the context of Jesus' proclamation of the Kingdom of God. This also explains more clearly how all the faithful share in Christ's priestly mission to teach, heal, and to glorify his Father.

We will now undertake to examine each of these missions in turn. We begin with the prophetic element of baptismal priesthood. This is about the witness of the lives of believers to the life of the Holy Spirit that is in them.

THE PROPHETIC ELEMENT

Jacques Maritain, an eminent Catholic philosopher, was captivated by the dream that lay Catholics would understand and relish the graced reality of a full Christian life. He wanted everybody to appreciate that a living faith and the joy of contemplation belong to them by reason of their baptism. Maritain and his wife, Raïssa, a poet, belonged to a group of distinguished Paris intellectuals who met for twenty years (1919–1939) to explore the theological basis for a fruitful Christian life in the world. In 1964, Maritain reflected back on that circle of friends and the fruits of their reflections:[4]

> The people [of God] are by definition a great and potent reserve of collective vitality. Their spontaneity, freedom of movement, and adaptability to the unexpected; their inventiveness and prophetic initiative, need to be fostered and respected as something sacred, even when all of that exists merely in a potential and undetermined state. . . .[5]

What a pity then that for so long—especially during the last four centuries—the Christian laity have believed themselves destined to imperfection, to a life of sin redeemed at the end, possibly, by a "happy death." They have cheerfully accepted this criminal dichotomy created by Baroque Catholicism. On the one hand, they have felt free to have all kinds of earthly pleasures devised by science and human wit . . . during this life here below, but then they imagined that afterwards the joys of heaven were reserved for only a small group of the predestined. . . .

If there is a single outstanding responsibility that should weigh upon the clergy of our time, it is to help the faithful escape from the damnable despair caused by this dichotomy and its paralyzing effects upon human history. Put it another way: the clergy have to help the faithful become aware of their vocation to share in the holiness of Jesus and his redemptive work, and how to "fill up what is lacking" (as to its application, not as to its merits) "to the passion of the Savior." (Col 1:24)[6]

Here Maritain was lamenting, on the one hand, the spiritual emptiness that is the inheritance of this "Baroque Catholicism" and, on the other hand, regretting the inert quality of lives that ought to be indispensable for an active Christian influence in the culture. A phrase that he frequently used for his dream of a living faith is *vivre l'évangile*—"to live the Gospel" which, of course, implies a life-giving relationship with Jesus as friend and master. He also used the term "prophetic" to describe the beneficial influence of faithful Christians upon other individuals and upon the culture as a whole.

For Maritain, the word *prophecy* refers not to an ability to foretell the future, the most common popular understanding of the word, but rather to a heightened sensitivity to the purposes or inspiration of God. In the Bible, the prophet is someone called to be a messenger of God. Prophets are also referred to as "seers." They are witnesses whose testimony is expressed both in words and in actions. Maritain uses prophecy in a generalized sense to mean a capacity to perceive and express God's hidden plan in one's social and cultural life. We will adopt that meaning of prophecy for our discussion of the prophetic element of baptismal priesthood.

Maritain's prophet has a penetrating curiosity about life and a strong bond of care for the destiny of others. The "prophetic" stance is the antithesis of the lifeless indifference toward the Kingdom of God that dominates consumer culture. Maritain thought that not only is every person endowed with a potential for a dynamic experience of God, but that this experience is necessary for an authentic human life. Lacking that spiritual rebirth, a person's life remains ultimately senseless.

Maritain deplored the generalized loss by the faithful of their spiritual birthright. In a strongly worded remark, he writes, "Among the laity (even those who are baptized), there are vast desert-like areas where it is more appropriate to refer to the 'unfaithful' rather than to the 'faithful.' Their faith, if it is really present after all, remains pathetically childish."[7] He meant this not as an insult, but in recognition of the fact that so many adult and otherwise sophisticated people never evolve beyond the concepts and language that they learned in childhood when expressing their religious ideas.

Maritain went on to insist, however, that despite all these difficulties, the age of the laity has arrived all the same. Writing in the 1960s, he was conscious not only of the initial impact of the thinking of the Second Vatican Council upon the church's self-understanding, but also of the writings and movements that prepared the way for the council by trying to draw the laity into the church's liturgy and into its social action in the world. He was confident that in time the lay faithful would become apostles of Christian faith in the full range of their interactions with others.

In the following citation, Maritain makes an interesting comparison between the cultural contribution to the local church by those in religious life and the potential role of an apostolic laity:

> For centuries, monasteries and religious houses have fulfilled the role [of providing a place of silence where God can be found], and they will not stop offering this service in the future. Whatever else may evolve to provide new opportunities of that kind, there will always be a need to deepen our spiritual experience in religious houses. However, my guess is that with the awakening of the Christian laity in our days we are observing a decisive transition in the history of the Church. Spiritual hospitality will also be practiced within the context of the lay world, at least in certain lay "prophetic minorities.". . . For years we have looked for it in all kinds of places: ashrams, houses of prayer, meditation centers, etc. Places like that are sources of spiritual renewal dispersed in the darkness of our human misery, and their influence will create new networks of faith and love on our poor earth.[8]

If we wonder how this idea of "spiritual hospitality" might be expressed in the busy lives of active Christians today, we can turn to some of the emerging forms of peer community that have developed in the U.S. church. The Christian Family Movement, Marriage Encounter, Teams of Our Lady, and other similar organizations for lay spiritual formation create cells or small base communities that exemplify Maritain's vision. These older movements that are expressions of small community have been around for quite a long time. More recently, however, some forms of parish renewal programs and parish retreats have been training parishioners in a similar way to continue the dynamics of the retreat program in small groups. In addition, some parishes and even dioceses, particularly in Latino cultural contexts, have organized Small Christian Communities to serve as the basic unit of parish experience and of Christian mutual support in faith and fellowship. All these are good examples of what Maritain was driving at, I think. And each of them has a powerful prophetic witness to contribute, not only to the participating members of the groups, but also to the wider parish and the wider society.

THE PROPHETIC CHARISM IN CONTEXT

How can the incompletely or vaguely instructed people whom Maritain called the "unfaithful" be transformed into a wise and dynamic people who can truly be designated as "prophetic"? "Faithful" really means faith-filled, which in turn means seeing how faith brings an abundance of meaning to everyday life. For faith-filled people, the providence of God resonates in their lives as a reality that helps them measure their judgments and their feelings. Such a vibrant faith has to be nurtured and sustained. Without this sense of God's presence and providence, their life in the church risks becoming just another routine, marginalized from their genuine priorities.

However, even without this kind of vital motivation, several factors keep many cradle Catholics in place within the church. Despite their failure to continue to learn about the church's theology, liturgy, spirituality, and culture after primary (or perhaps secondary) school, many still feel like the Catholic world is part of their family and social identity. That can be a very good thing; but it can also be a distraction from the real need for adult Christians to arrive at forming an adult faith.

Graduates of Catholic colleges or universities will almost surely have taken several courses in religious studies (sometimes under sufferance). But it would be fairly rare for such input to become a genuine intellectual foundation in Christian faith, mainly because the insights of these courses are seldom integrated with learning from the rest of the curriculum. Still, family bonds often hold people in a Catholic social network even when their religious practice does not intellectually make sense. A hunger for religious experience and the reassuring comfort of familiar rituals draw many back. The sheer force of habit coupled with subtle feelings of guilt at abandoning childhood religious practices keep others in place.

As we already noted, the U.S. church is growing in numbers for a variety of different reasons. Church growth suggests of itself healthy religion. How strange, then, that a recent document of the Bishops' Conference would have to admit: "Many Catholics seem 'lukewarm' in faith . . . or have a limited understanding of what the Church believes, teaches, and lives."[9] There can be little doubt that much will be required to generate a prophetic spirit in the baptized "unfaith-filled." But at least this issue is on the table in a new way as a result of the bishops' document.

One obvious question has to be, "Why is there a gap between people's general culture and their religious culture?" The real issue may not be complete indifference, but rather what frank, colloquial language today calls a "disconnect." I often try to calm down my students at the start of a course in theology by telling them that the world is unequally divided into two categories of thinkers—"theologians" and "earth people"—and that the goal of our course will be to translate the theologians' message into earth people talk. It is not easy, but it is an issue. People who feel competent in their social and professional roles can feel embarrassed or uncomfortable with biblical or theological enquiry because it falls outside their experience.

For example, here is an observation that goes back twenty-five years and is still daunting to someone who tries to preach at Sunday Mass and teach Christian theology. These lines come from a diary of the writer, Henri Nouwen, which he kept during a year-long monastic experience at a Trappist monastery in upstate New York:

> For the past few weeks we have had a Friday night lecture by a visiting seminary professor. He has been speaking about the doctrine of the Trinity and especially about the Holy Spirit. For me these lectures are a special experience. . . . I like the lectures, I am intrigued, I don't want to miss them—but at the same time I feel dissatisfied on a level I did not understand in the past but is now closer to my consciousness . . . I kept saying to myself, "How

interesting, how insightful"—and at the same time I said to myself, "So what? What do all these words about God the Father, the Son, and the Spirit have to do with [people] here and now?" As soon as I step outside the circle of his terminology, which is very familiar to me, the whole level of discourse seems extremely alienating.[10]

In other words, conversations about God, church, spirituality, and human destiny must take place today in a new context that is different from the mental and symbolic worlds of Jesus, the evangelists, early church theologians, medieval religious writers, great mystics, leaders of the Protestant Reformation, the Pilgrims, or even our grandparents. For all of them, the idea of evolution would have been unimaginable, replaced instead by the divine action of creation; the curative action of miracle drugs was unknown, healing came from an intervention of divine mercy; the power of a volcano, an earthquake, or a hurricane would have been explained not by tectonic plates or equatorial winds, but by God's will.

Scriptural modes of expression are permeated with a strong sense of direct divine causality and immediate divine presence in the world. Convictions about the proximity of God's power to touch and control our lives can become a jarring obstacle to educated adults who have studied hard to understand the achievements of modern science and contemporary technology. We have not forgotten how in the seventeenth century Vatican authorities required Galileo to publicly repudiate the new knowledge that empirical scientific learning had shown him about our solar system.

But that defensive scenario won't work today. Instead of asking Catholic scholars, scientists, and people of influence to withdraw from the cutting edge of scientific progress, the church today must appeal to these leaders in the culture to become interpreters of the Christian mysteries to the cultured skeptics who are their peers. In fact, the Council, at least, did dream out loud about just such a learned influence from the robust faith of Christian scholars and scientists in the forum of both academic and general cultural settings.

Twenty years before Henri Nouwen, just before Vatican II, Yves Congar reflected on the impasse between theology and our technological world as a concern for the church. In his words:

What has happened is the emergence of a profane, "not sacred," world, a world of technology; and inevitably, from the very nature of their sacred calling, the clergy are out of contact with such a world. They were quite at home in the world which, at bottom, the church had shaped, the forms of whose existence were more or less of the same kind as those in the traditional church; but this is no longer so. The clergy cannot, or only with the greatest difficulty, be at home in a world that is wholly secular, technological, and infatuated with [this] earth. On this Ascension Day in the year of grace 1958, people are more interested in Sputnik III than in the Lord whom Christians worship.[11]

In the opening chapters above, we saw clearly how much the vision of the Constitution on the Church focused upon the evangelizing power of the laity to carry the yeast of the Gospel into the world: "Only through them can the church be salt and light for the world" (LG 33). Yet in the forty years since the council, considerably more emphasis has been put upon liturgical legislation than upon adult faith formation for evangelization.[12] In recent years, Vatican documents touching the liturgy have too often conveyed either explicitly or implicitly the conviction of their authors that the liturgy belongs to the ordained, and that we must above all attend to a proper etiquette in its performance. The particular question at issue may be translation, preaching, degrees of participation, who has access to the sanctuary, or something else. But rare indeed in such documents on liturgical directives is any reference to the missionary calling of the baptized.

As we focus on the prophetic element in baptismal priesthood we must, on the one hand, reaffirm the missionary vocation of the faithful and, on the other hand, create a thorough adult faith formation or mystagogy. Happily, experience shows us that the missionary instinct flows quite naturally from the heart of those who have learned the mystery of Christ.

FAITH: GOING BEYOND WORDS

The fundamental meaning of the prophetic element of baptismal priesthood is that a person becomes a sign of new life as a member of Christ's body in the world. The Scriptures speak of this sign value in these terms: "the fruit of the Spirit is love, joy, peace, patience, kindness. . ." (cf. Gal 5:22). The spiritual life overflows into social presence and action. This new quality of life requires an understanding of the paschal mystery of Christ and a willing gift of self to the dynamics of conversion. "Those who belong to Christ Jesus have crucified the flesh with its passions and desires" (Gal 5:24). Faith is a call to unceasing conversion and transformation, calling the self beyond itself.

The grace of Christ's priesthood overflows into every dimension of human experience giving new meaning to our lives and our actions as Christians. Christ offers to the Father his members' obedience of faith. Their acts of submission to the Holy Spirit—their docility of faith and their discipline of self-control—transform them into disciples. They sacrifice their willful egotism and they seek to be led by the Spirit out of love and desire for God. This life of Christian faith becomes linked to the priestly offering Christ makes to his Father. It expresses the self-offering of his members sharing in his priesthood.

The Christian faith is complex: it is not just about ideas, but about a kind of new life. Faith cannot be only about saying words. Reciting the Creed, despite the words "I believe," is not the same thing as believing. Faith requires a connection between the words of the church's creeds and our hunger for meaning, belonging, affirmation, forgiveness, empowerment, and happiness. When that synthesis is achieved, then transformation begins.

Faith is a new language that is deeper than the words and texts handed down by generations of Christ's disciples. Above all it is expressed in interior acts or attitudes of abandonment to what we have been calling here the Spirit's anointing. Faith is first of all surrender, then prophecy. I accept the tradition's witness in its Creed; then I affirm my faith by living it in the power of the Holy Spirit.

The nineteenth century English theologian, Cardinal John Henry Newman, sought to describe mature faith to the cultured adults of his time. He devised a helpful conceptual tool, namely, his distinction between the "notional" and the "real."[13] For Newman, notional assent is superficial and abstract—little more than assertions made out of habit. Newman contrasted this notional assent with real assent. If notional assent means saying *yes* to an idea, real assent means saying *yes* to something we have actually experienced.

Newman observed that even the great doctrines of Christian religion—that there is a God, that God has certain attributes, and that God has revealed the divine will—all this can be the subject of notional assent, to the degree that it remains at the level of abstractions or vague, general ideas. People may imagine that they are fully engaged in Christian practice when, in fact, they have never yet come to grips with the surrender that divine faith requires.

The visible paraphernalia of religion—religious texts, ritual actions, institutional structures, etc.—all refer to God and celebrate God, but they are incapable in themselves of giving us a real experience of God. The beauty, complexity, and wisdom of the religious apparatus can be all consuming. But if it remains in the area of notions or ideas, as such, it stays disconnected from ourselves.

Getting beyond the notional into the real, ironically, means leaving the visible and embarking on a journey into the invisible. This means going from religion to faith, from ritual to mystery, and from self-concern to loss of self. The only tour guide for that journey, as we have suggested before in chapter 3, is God's Holy Spirit.

Prophets have a role in helping people take this risk of moving beyond ideas and rituals into experiences and commitments. As those who strive to live in the power of the Holy Spirit, prophets reshape the meaning of events and opportunities by the way they speak and live. By forming the faithful to be prophets through its preaching and its community life, the church has the potential capacity to transform society by transforming the way people look at the world around them as reflected in the lives of these prophets.

Let's look at another way of talking about this need to go beyond superficial assent. God speaks to us in two ways, both of them essential to our spiritual well being. I will call them the "exterior word" and the "interior word." God speaks with an exterior word through the church's theological and cultural tradition. Scripture itself, insofar as it is a written text, is an exterior word, as are the texts of the liturgical books, the works of great theologians, the preaching of the church's ministers, and any other cultural residue of a believer's living experience of faith. The exterior word conveys what Newman might call a notional understanding and leads to notional assent. Such exterior, notional evidence points toward God and invites faith in God, but the awakening of that faith requires something else besides the exterior word.

The witness of the exterior word is essential, of course. The truth of the Sacred Scriptures is definitive. But it can nonetheless remain merely words exterior to the human heart. An example can make this clear. Two persons can hear at the same time and in the same place the proclamation of God's revealed word, both in the Scriptures proclaimed and in the preaching of a minister, and one will be led to faith and praise and the other remain skeptical and withdrawn. The exterior word is exactly the same for them both, but something else makes a profound difference in their response.

In order for the church's tradition expressed in the exterior word to become life-giving and fruitful, there must be an interior word. This happens when a person "hears" or experiences an anointing of the Holy Spirit and is led to faith. This is seldom a dramatic or eso- teric event. It often has more of the quality of an "aha" moment. The Holy Spirit acts in harmony with the psychology of normal life. God alone is able to touch us at the very depths of our being, at that core of ourselves from which understanding and assent arise.

The Spirit's touch or influence upon our powers of understanding and love does not feel like the intrusion of a foreign element, but like a deepening (or even an awakening) of our sensibilities. The church has always had a clear tradition that such a gift or influence from God is required for an authentic response of faith. As the Vatican Coun- cil's Dogmatic Constitution on Divine Revelation (n. 8) puts it, "The Holy Spirit, through whom the living voice of the Gospel rings out in the Church—and through it in the world—leads believers to the full truth and makes the word of Christ dwell in them in all its richness" (see Col 3:16).

Looking at someone's surrender of faith with hindsight, we may be able to discover points of engagement with personal, aesthetic, or intellectual interests that seem to have led this person to the submis- sion of his or her life to God. However, movements of faith flow out of trust and love. They are not the conclusion of a reasoned argu- ment. Just as the most powerful loves in our life can never be logi- cally accounted for, so also the faith commitments in our lives remain mysteriously beyond any full accounting.

This is an area where example and evocation are more telling than argumentation. Often, scientifically formed, competent adults have over time built protective barriers against the intrusion of mystery in their lives. So it takes an ambush to break through those defenses and create a psychic experience that leads them to hunger for further explanation.

Some prophets express themselves most powerfully through art or literature. When people become aware of the reality of the Spirit's ac- tion in their lives, they often turn to poetry rather than prose, to image rather than argument, to express what they feel happening to them. In this vein, here is a poem by Thomas Merton that evokes some of the power of the interior word as we have described it:

When psalms surprise me with their music
And antiphons turn to rum
The Spirit sings: the bottom drops out of my soul . . .
And I go forth with no more wine and no more stars
And no more buds and no more Eden
And no more animals and no more sea:

While God sings by himself in acres of night
And walls fall down, that guarded Paradise.[14]

The poet confesses a kind of blessed bewilderment about what has happened to him ("psalms surprise me . . ."). He has experienced the joy
of the presence of God in his life, but cannot say just how it happened
("the bottom drops out of my soul . . ."). He evokes the beauty and
majesty of the God whom he meets in faith ("While God sings by himself in acres of night. . . ."), but must simply allow that there is nothing more that he can say. So he reevaluates his understanding of what is
going on ("walls fall down, that guarded Paradise").

Merton's phrase, "the bottom drops out of my soul," reminds me
a lot of Paul's phrase in Romans, "the Spirit speaks in sighs too deep
for words" (8:26). In both, only a metaphor conveys the conviction
that the invisible God is present and active, in the one case, exploding
the complacency of self-possession and, in the other, refocusing our
knowing to make it inclusive of the Spirit's hidden action in our lives.
For some of us, the arts are the most effective form of sharing such
experiences, although for others the task of rational explanation will
always be a duty and passion.

Turning back to Maritain's interest in prophecy as a fertile element
in the world of culture, we can note that he named as prophets the
novelists Dostoyevsky and Bernanos, the poets Péguy and Baudelaire,
and even the anti-Christian philosopher Nietzsche. To explain himself, he said: "I think that certain poets and certain great writers can
articulate for the world a kind of prophetic sense alive in the hearts of
the faithful."[15] For him, the prophetic instinct was not something
given exclusively to good Christians: "there are many more graces in
the world than we might think." By sizing up the powerful forces at
work in the mind and hearts of their contemporaries, these "prophets"
shape a response in faith from believers who care deeply about the
world's salvation. Evidently this kind of prophecy implies profound
attentiveness to what is going on in the spirits of one's neighbors and
countrymen.

The most concise way to describe what prophecy means is to call it divine communication through a human person. As we saw in chapter 3, Jesus' prophetic role was linked to his entire life, not just to his words and miracles. In a parallel way, the prophetic element in the lives of his disciples embraces their whole lives. The lives of Christians rooted in faith speak for the kingdom of God. Do we all need to be poets? Of course not. Do we all need to be prophets of social change? No. But a life transformed by the power of the Spirit must, and will, bear witness to the One who transforms it.

Here we have stressed at great length the transforming power of faith in God so as to convey how a radical change in the disciple's heart is necessary if the prophetic message is going to be true. Remember how much emphasis Jesus placed upon this reality in his preaching: "You are the salt of the earth; but if salt has lost its taste, how can its saltiness be restored? . . . You are the light of the world. A city built on a hill cannot be hid" (Matt 5:13, 14).

Today's U.S. church is being transformed by the generous involvement of Lay Ecclesial Ministers in the apostolic works of the parish. Since Maritain wrote in the late 1950s and early 1960s about the prophetic potential of the laity, official statements of the church exhorting the laity to apostolic action have multiplied. Even more significant has been the extraordinary growth of new roles for lay ministers working alongside priests and bishops. As we noted in chapter 1, there are now approximately equal numbers of Ecclesial Lay Ministers and ordained priests working in parish ministries. With about as many faithful in graduate and formation programs for professional lay ministry as already working in the field, we may reasonably anticipate in the near future that the ratio of lay to ordained ministers will even increase.

This situation imposes upon us the need to answer a number of important questions regarding academic preparation, spiritual formation, professional relationships to the bishop and diocese, just compensation and job security, commissioning and instituting of ecclesial lay ministers. Many of these issues are explored in considerable depth in a fine new book edited by Susan Wood entitled *Ordering the Baptismal Priesthood*.[16] Such questions are not examined here because of our broader interest in the phenomenon of the priesthood of the faithful in any and all contexts, not just formal ministerial roles. The focus here, a perspective that will be extended into the following chapters, is upon understanding all forms of apostolic witness of the faithful as an expression of their baptismal priesthood.

Most serious Christians will not be living out their baptismal priesthood within a commissioned lay ministry; rather it will be in the workplace, family, and networks of relationships in which they live their ordinary lives. Some points of engagement for fruitful and faithful witness include those between one member of a couple and the other, between parents and children, and among neighbors in their frequent interactions in their homes and neighborhoods. We need to appreciate the dynamic importance of just such encounters in the lives of the faithful.

Sociologists have asserted that the United States, which began with very strong grass-roots structures for cooperation, has of late lost many forms of its "social capital."[17] Social capital refers to the regular exchanges among family, friends, and neighbors that offer support, reinforcement of values, and incentives to social action. It is easy to imagine that the living faith of adult Christians might reinvigorate structures of social capital as a byproduct of awakening consciousness about the power of faith in action. As we build contacts and commitments for the expression of faith in social situations, we build Christian social capital. As we talk about and engage the cooperation of others in our hopes for more vital community, we build structures of mutual commitment.

Much has been written in recent years about faith in the marketplace, and all that pertains to the prophetic element.[18] Explaining the prophetic element in the workplace and politics is complex, but we can begin with this equation: Christian prophecy in society = responsibility + obedience of faith. There is no escaping the demands of justice and integrity, but there is also no escaping the Christian *extra* which is a kind of "integrity-plus."

Let me try to explain my idea in steps. It seems to me that there are at least these five aspects to what we have been calling the prophetic element:

(a) thorough competence: preparedness for the job, readiness to respond to the demands of the roles one takes on
(b) whole-heartedness: willingness to invest one's gifts to the full with genuineness and sincerity
(c) personal lucidity about the life of faith linked to a vocation— one recognizes oneself called to faith and called into service according to the talents and desires of one's heart

(d) an intention to serve the kingdom of God: aiming at making a contribution with one's life that will build human solidarity for the sake of social communion with God; the New Testament calls it "building up the body of Christ"

(e) a desire to share the blessings of a living relationship with God through Christ in the Holy Spirit; desiring to bring others to faith and into communion.

Competence, whole-heartedness, vocation, intention, and desire—these five elements together constitute the prophetic element of a fruitful Christian life.

There is a spectrum of ways in which the faithful approach these aspects of the prophetic element: from very conscious to hardly conscious of the values involved; from very explicit to hardly explicit about one's Christian intention; and from closely linked to hardly linked to explicit Catholic communities and/or programs. The plotting of a particular niche on this matrix of forces will depend upon the maturity and intensity of faith of the individual, the nature of the context in which one works, and the depth of the relationship that binds people together. Even if in some cases Christians have only a poor awareness or a weak intention, their impact upon society cannot be neutral. Social interaction either reinforces or dissolves the values that people share (explicitly or implicitly), including the value of faith and divine vocation.

There are many serious Christians whose lives are brilliant expressions of what we just called "the Christian *extra*—integrity-plus": parents who hunger to hand on to their children a life-giving faith; spouses who grow together through the inevitable pains and struggles of marriage out of a conviction that they have been called by God to find their holiness with one another; executives, workers, and community builders whose hunger for justice springs out of love for the poor based on a radical listening to the words of Jesus; Ecclesial Lay Ministers whose passion for the mission of the church has led them to take on incredibly demanding jobs for salaries that are embarrassingly inadequate. All these are exemplary expressions of the priesthood that were given to them in their baptism and which Christ offers in their name to his Father. Their fidelity and patience in seeking to link the ordinary experiences of their lives with their graced vocation and destiny is their way of moving more fully from a notional to a real experience of Christ's paschal mystery.

MOVING ON

Having now reflected at length on the prophetic element of the baptismal priesthood, we will be moving on to explore two more of its elements: the pastoral or "royal" mission, and the cultic or "priestly" mission. Much of the foundation we have laid in this chapter is common to all three of these missions, so rest assured the going will be somewhat easier from here on.

As we saw, Maritain dreamed that lay Catholics would have the opportunity to cherish the reality of a full Christian life. I dream that those who are already giving the full measure of their life and talents to the service of the kingdom of God will come to know the meaning of the baptismal priesthood in their lives. As they live prophetically in Christian faith anointed by the Holy Spirit, they should know that they already share through their priestly action a foretaste of the eternal friendship that will be theirs, "face to face," when they are finally one with Christ their head in heaven. They have become channels of love and grace, empowered by Christ who needs them. They have become effective and vital expressions of a priestly people.

In our day, the new situation of Christians in a post-Christian world requires both greater creativity and greater generosity. The shaping of priorities for political communities and for families and neighborhoods has been passed on to the faithful in the sense that they can accept or refuse the decisions that their leaders propose to them, and they can take initiatives to infuse the surrounding culture with the life of faith. Those culture-shaping decisions are not, for the most part, dramatic and self-conscious events; rather, they are often the result of small choices and expressions of attitude in the flux of day-to-day living. Choosing well and with clear commitment to Christian values is a prophetic task in the present day. Such prophecy shapes individuals, families, parishes, and ultimately whole communities. Only the laity are positioned to express that influence in today's society. Only through them can the church be salt and light in the reshaping of the culture.

Notes

1. Lucien Deiss, *Springtime of the Liturgy: Liturgical Texts of the First Four Centuries*, trans. Matthew J. O'Connell (Collegeville: The Liturgical Press, 1979) 132. The extraordinary influence of this early text on twentieth century liturgical reforms as well as doubts raised by recent scholarship about its putative author and provenance are discussed in a recent essay: John F. Baldovin, "Hippolytus and the *Apostolic Tradition*: Recent Research and Commentary," *Theological Studies* 64:3 (2003) 520–42.

2. Yves Congar, "Sur la Trilogie: Prophète-Roi-Prêtre," *Revue des sciences philosophiques et théologiques* 67 (1983) 97–115. Cf. John Calvin, *Institutes of the Christian Religion* II, 15.

3. Ibid., 112 (translation is mine).

4. Jacques Maritain, *Carnet de Notes* (Paris: Desclée de Brouwer, 1965) 183f. (translation is mine).

5. Ibid., 241–2.

6. Ibid., 243.

7. Ibid., 250–1.

8. Ibid., 252–3.

9. *Our Hearts Were Burning Within Us: A Pastoral Plan for Adult Faith Formation in the United States* (Washington, DC: United States Catholic Conference, 1999) §35.

10. Henri Nouwen, *Genesee Diary* (Garden City: Doubleday, 1976) 149, 150.

11. Yves Congar, *Laity, Church and World*, trans. Donald Atwater (Baltimore: Helicon Press, 1960) 65.

12. Note should be made of the exception of several high profile writings of Pope John Paul II: *Redemptoris Missio, Catechesi Tradendae,* and *Christifideles Laici*; as well as of the important encyclical of Pope Paul VI, *Evangelii Nuntiandi*. All of these documents lay some stress on lay apostolic witness.

13. John Henry Newman, *An Essay in Aid of a Grammar of Assent* (Garden City, NY: Doubleday/Image Book, 1955) ch. 4.

14. Thomas Merton, *Selected Poems of Thomas Merton* (New York: New Directions, 1967) 84.

15. Maritain, op. cit., 247.

16. Susan K. Wood, ed., *Ordering the Baptismal Priesthood: Theologies of Lay and Ordained Ministries* (Collegeville: Liturgical Press, 2003).

17. See, e.g., Robert D. Putnam, *Bowling Alone: The Collapse and Revival of American Community* (New York: Simon & Schuster, 2000).

18. The most emphatic expression in this regard to come from the universal magisterium of the church was the Apostolic Exhortation *Christifideles Laici* (The Lay Members of Christ's Faithful People) 1988, by Pope John Paul II. The Apostolic Exhortation of Pope Paul VI *Evangelii Nuntiandi* (On Evangelization in the Modern World) 1975, treats similar themes of effective lay witness.

Chapter 6

Hearts Set
on the Kingdom of God

Bob and Janet have been married for twenty years, have two teenage children, a lovely suburban household, and all the stresses of conscientious busy people. In mid-career as project director for an ecology laboratory, Bob often feels suffocated by the routine of his work and wishes he could break out and find a more interesting life. Janet teaches English at the university and wonders each year if her students are actually coming less prepared for college work, or if she is becoming less resilient herself. Both Bob and Janet feel at times as though their work is drudgery and wonder about the meaning of it all.

Their children are both in high school. The older son, Colin, is getting ready for college and looking forward to the independence of life away from home. The younger daughter, Meg, is beginning to dream of a future as a lawyer, and is working really hard at school in order to make herself competitive. She sees herself in every episode of "L.A. Law." These two teenage children have become quite disinterested in Sunday Mass and only attend under pressure at this point. "Why do we keep going?" they sometimes ask, when it is evident that their parents are frustrated by the disappointing preaching that they occasionally hear at church.

Here are four good people, and four egos struggling to find recognition and meaning for their life projects. What can hold them together as a family? What can provide them the motivation they need to grow strong in their integrity?

On the other side of town, Maria is a widowed mother who works part-time in order to keep her family together. She has two small children, Juanito and Teresita. Her husband Juan was killed in Iraq last year, and she is still numb about her loss even while feeling driven to work as much as she can to survive economically. The five affluent families for whom she does domestic service are friendly and sympathetic. But Maria feels like she's on a race track, chasing herself through days of hard work away from home and of demanding attention to her two children when she is back in her own house. Maria is devout and faithful to Sunday Mass. She is teaching her two little ones to pray, at least at table and at bedtime. But she herself is searching to understand what God wants from her and she's restless because her life feels so incomplete without her husband. What can help Maria find peace and happiness in her troubled life?

These families are every family in a way. Some families are financially better off, others not so well off. Some are more socially involved, others less so. But most families are coping with these same typical stresses and challenges: calibrating spousal intimacy, nurturing and spiritually forming their children, attending to the personal hungers of each member, and wondering what the ultimate outcome of their efforts will be. These issues are even harder to handle under more difficult circumstances like unemployment, family violence, alcohol or drug abuse, or mental illness. But challenges like those of Janet and Bob and even like those of Maria and her children are the inescapable problems that every family—and every person—has to wrestle with.

These are the raw materials of a life of consecrated Christian sacrifice. In each instance, the person has an opportunity to identify his or her life with the redeeming sacrifice of Christ. The hunger for acceptance and belonging, the generosity of parents in patiently supporting their children through ups and downs, the anxiety of struggling to understand God's will in the midst of frustration or fatigue—all of this can only find lasting meaning and authentic resolution in Christian experience.

As we begin to explore the royal mission of Christ's priesthood as it is shared by the faithful, we can begin to see the importance of the theme of vocation in the Christian life. All of these persons, parents and children, have a vocation to intimacy with God in the midst of their seemingly chaotic lives. A vocation means that God calls a person to discipleship with Jesus, shapes that person through the gifts of the Holy Spirit, and enables that person to realize himself or herself through acting in accord with the vision of the Gospel. Let's look and see why this admixture of elements is related to the royal dimension of Christ's priesthood, and what that really means.

THE SPIRIT OF CHRIST'S KINGSHIP

The words *king* and *kingdom* often stir up images of power and hierarchy. Most of human history has been recorded in terms of the military struggles of earthly kingdoms. Even in our age of democracy, the bias of the world's strongest leaders is to control rather than to cooperate, as the example of the U.S. invasion of Iraq sadly illustrates. It is important, therefore, to be clear that the kingship of Christ has radically transformed the concept of king, just as the priesthood of Christ has transformed the idea of priesthood.

A passage of supreme significance in the New Testament is found in Mark 10. In responding to the request of James and John for privileged positions in the kingdom of God, Jesus utters words that overturn the impulsive inclination to competition that so easily captivates our minds and hearts:

> So Jesus called them and said to them, "You know that among the Gentiles those whom they recognize as their rulers lord it over them, and their great ones are tyrants over them. But it is not so among you; but whoever wishes to become great among you must be your servant, and whoever wishes to be first among you must be slave of all. For the Son of Man came not to be served but to serve, and to give his life as a ransom for many." (Mark 10:42-45)

The one who would be great in God's kingdom will become the servant of all. Implicit in this revelation is the promise of the Holy Spirit to illuminate and strengthen Jesus' disciples as they strive to follow his attitudes and actions. Jesus' insistence on loving service of others as the fundamental attitude of his followers can be read clearly not only here in Mark 10 and in the parallel passages in Matthew (20:24-28) and Luke (22:24-27), but also and especially in John 13, where the washing of his disciples' feet and his command to wash one another's feet is linked to the very meaning of the Eucharist.

Unlike the other three Gospels, John does not give us the words of the institution narrative ("this is my body; this is my blood . . .") in his account of the Last Supper. John's Gospel does not speak of the "symbolic matter" and "graced sign," as we have called these elements, but only of the "realized mystery." He shows us that mystery fulfilled in a graphic display of love and service, and then narrates these words of the Lord: "If I, your Lord and Teacher, have washed your feet, you also ought to wash one another's feet. For I have set you an example, that you also should do as I have done to you" (John 13:14-15).

In all these passages, Jesus overturns society's presumption of competitive dominance as an acceptable style of social interaction. He disarms James and John's struggle for dominance, as he does in other places by teaching the disciples an ethic of transforming love. He systematically refuses to allow individual self-interest to disfigure the communion of humble obedience to God's call and the unity of the emerging community of the disciples. Jesus rejects utilitarian relationships with others; his strong message for our moment of history might be phrased as a maxim in these words: love persons, use things; not vice versa. Each person is precious—a sacrament of divine creative love, and for that reason worthy of respect. A person can never be a means to egoistic ends.[1]

When the Gospel of John comes finally to identify Jesus with the title of king, it does so in an episode of ironic reversal. Although Jesus is defeated in political and physical terms by the kingdom of Caesar and the powers of this world, his defeat is the inception of his paschal triumph that will lead to his eternal kingship in the life of resurrection. John's Gospel tells the story in detail:

> Then Pilate . . . summoned Jesus, and asked him, "Are you the king of the Jews?" . . . Jesus answered, "My kingdom is not from this world. If my kingdom were from this world, my followers would be fighting to keep me from being handed over . . . But as it is, my kingdom is not from here?" Pilot asked him, "So you are a king?" Jesus answered, "You say that I am a king. For this I was born, and for this I came into the world, to testify to the truth. Everyone who belongs to the truth listens to my voice." (John 18:33-37)

As king, Jesus in no way denies the ethic of self-giving service that he taught so earnestly. Rather, he illustrates the meaning of his power as king in the gift of his life for others in his cruel suffering and terrible death. Jesus' kingship belongs to his post-resurrection ministry at the right hand of the Father, just as his priesthood does. He offers to the Father his struggle against the violent and greedy powers of this world that led him to his sacrificial death. But above all, he offers his triumph over these powers in his resurrection body, of which the faithful have become a part as his members.

Here is the meaning of the kingly mission of the faithful as they share their Lord's priesthood. They offer to the Father along with Jesus their combat against the powers of this world, against selfish competitiveness that discounts the needs and concerns of others, against consumerism that reduces human value to expensive passing acts of self-indulgence, and against pornography and dehumanizing manipulation that appeal to the grossest animal instincts of tired and wounded people.

All the pain, patience, and ambiguity that arise from such struggles are a genuine engagement with evil. Overcoming the forces of evil in such instances focuses and strengthens the faithful to establish a kingdom of justice and love in their own lives by reason of their solidarity with Christ through their presence of mind and their growing strength of will. Out of this royal priestly mission emerges both a more mature disciple and a visible witness to the kingdom of God.

THE ROYAL MISSION OF THE COMMON PRIESTHOOD

In his apostolic exhortation on the laity, Pope John Paul II summarizes the meaning of the royal mission of the priesthood of the baptized as follows:

> Because the lay faithful belong to Christ . . . they share in his kingly mission and are called by him to spread that kingdom in history. They exercise their kingship as Christians, above all, in the spiritual combat in which they seek to overcome in themselves the kingdom of sin. . . , and then to make a gift of themselves so as to serve, in justice and in charity, Jesus who is himself present in all his brothers and sisters, above all in the very least. (cf. Matt 25:40)[2]

Pope John Paul repeats here an emphasis that is found in the theology of St. Thomas Aquinas with reference to the meaning of the priesthood of the baptized. In his various writings, St. Thomas points out that the spiritual sacrifices of the baptized are distinguished from "external" sacrifices or objects. The spiritual sacrifice is always in some respect an offering of one's very self.[3] For this offering to be worthy, the faithful must undertake the discipline of bringing about in their own lives the harmony and integrity that are the achievement of moral maturity and virtue.

Put another way, the acceptable self-offering is that of a person who is always changing, being transformed by faith and love and by the gifts of the Holy Spirit into a worthy sacrament of the Body of Christ. We can all offer our ongoing conversion to a deeper Christian life as the fundamental spiritual sacrifice of our priesthood.

In St. Thomas's understanding of the priestly offering of the faithful, there is a sense in which they offer a sacrificial "holocaust." This word means the complete and absolute offering of their own selves as a willing act of thanksgiving to God to whom they owe the whole of their existence.[4] What is entailed here is a highly refined understanding of the foundational meaning of Christian existence. The Bible teaches us that life itself is a gift from God. Through the ages, the church's theology has understood that gift not as an event in the past, but as an ever-present gift from Creator to creature. God will communicate divine life as fully as the creature is capable of receiving it. To that extent, the story of any Christian's life is the story of repeatedly growing into readiness to receive divine gifts.

And so we are called to grow in self-control, justice, authentic moral imagination, and mindfulness. All the dynamics of Christian moral and religious practice have as their aim the development of a person who is more and more finely attuned to the gifts and the guidance of the Holy Spirit. The practices of the Christian life remove obstacles like rebellion, ignorance, self-preoccupation, and apathy so as to increase a person's readiness to respond to grace. In a healthy Christian life, religious practices running the spectrum from Sunday Eucharist to daily acts of self-sacrifice for the sake of others are undertaken with joy and alacrity because they are seen as part of the normal growth of the person into a Christ-like generosity.

Later we will see some of the ways in which Christian adults come to a mature understanding of their faith and its demands. But you can begin to understand how the knowledge and acceptance of a Christian understanding of human maturity is linked to Christ's rule as our spiritual king. We will also point out that in the actual state of affairs in today's church, the spiritual formation of adults in this kind of discipline will thrive more effectively in small group experiences than in individual efforts to learn and grow in isolation.

Pope John Paul continues his description of the royal mission of the faithful as follows:

In particular the lay faithful are called to restore to creation all its original value. In ordering creation to the authentic well-being of humanity in an activity governed by the life of grace, they share in the exercise of the power with which the Risen Christ draws all things to himself and subjects them along with himself to the Father, so that God might be everything to everyone . . .[5]

If Christians live in the Spirit and develop a spiritual maturity that intentionally seeks to place their lives at the service of the kingdom of God, if their hearts grow large with compassion for a world seeking lasting love and their minds expansive with a vision of justice and peace for all people, then they will devote their energies to sharing the good news of Christ's kingdom. Christ's mandate for us is to work for the growth of the new creation—a world where God's purposes are expressed as a result of our obedience of faith. Pope John Paul describes this same reality as a call "to restore to creation all its original value."

The theological link here, of course, is the role of human intelligence in the context of material creation. Humans are in many senses the intelligence and executives of the physical world. Through our understanding, science, and technology, we develop plans and programs that harness not only our own energies, but also the energies of the animal and physical world to our purposes. To utilize this enormous power, not for selfish and hedonistic purposes, but for the real common good of all peoples and of the planet as well is to "share in the exercise of the power with which the Risen Christ draws all things to himself and subjects them along with himself to the Father. . . ," as Pope John Paul puts it above.

In the U.S. church we have not done too good a job of explaining this link between human work and the divine plan, between the economy and our possibilities for fostering a new creation, or between personal discipline in a consumer society and our shared responsibility for the common good of all people. Despite more than a century of articulate and challenging church documents that clearly elaborate Catholic social teaching, not too much Sunday preaching is heard in parishes about economic justice, concern for the unemployed and the poor, or the New Testament's vision of justice as a participation in God's care for all of humanity. Yet all these dimensions of social and economic life are closely linked to the royal mission of the priesthood of the faithful.[6] When these themes are meaningfully addressed in preaching, great numbers of the faithful of the parish take them to heart. In this way, the royal charism of the faithful becomes a living reality in the parish and often finds expression in apostolic works touching the economic and political orders.

I hope that clarifying the meaning of the baptismal priesthood for the church's faithful will lead to their understanding their dignity and duty as stewards of God's merciful justice in a world that has gone mad in its unhampered lust for wealth and power over others. The ruling spirit of Christ's authority is very different from the practices of the competitive capitalistic world in which we live.

BUILDING UP THE CHURCH WITHIN THE FAMILY

So far we have seen that the royal mission of Christ's priesthood as shared by the faithful bears upon their taking life in hand with a view to responding generously to their vocation as disciples of the Lord. This provides them with meaning and motivation for the difficulties of their own lives and the sacrifices that these entail. It also sustains them in their courageous acceptance of life's challenges for the sake of bearing witness to their Lord in the world. This is a theology of corporate life, as we have so often noted—the life of the Body of Christ.

Vatican II's Decree on the Laity suggests that families need to help one another to understand and address their sacramental potential as disciples and witnesses to the Lordship of Christ. It says: "To attain the ends of their apostolate more easily it can be of advantage for families to organize themselves into groups."[7] One might go so far as to say that without some sort of group support it is hard to see how couples and families could ever hope to thrive in their Christian faith and witness.

This advice of the Decree on the Laity flows from a principle of central importance that is often overlooked. No one can be expected to live the Christian life without help from other members of the Body of Christ. In fact, one of the primary motives for St. Paul in developing his powerful metaphor of the Body of Christ, employed in his letters to the Corinthians, Romans, and Galatians, was to communicate to the new members of these early churches their vital dependence upon one another in order to help them grow in faith and mutual service. Human nature has not changed since the first century; we still need to help one another believe, deepen our convictions, and grow in generosity.

In some of the earlier chapters, we made note of the U.S. Bishops' Pastoral Plan for Adult Faith Formation. In that plan, there is a good practical description of ways in which couples and families as well as single adults can provide mutual support for growth in faith and discipleship in the context of the Catholic parish. The document acknowledges the need to promote a "linkage between the faith we profess and celebrate and the life we live, thus meeting one of the principal challenges of our day."[8] In a systematic way, the bishops' document describes five approaches that can contribute to ongoing faith formation. All of these approaches address the need for adult Catholics to develop through experience a better understanding of the church's authentic teaching as it applies to the nuts and bolts of their daily lives.

The first approach describes the ways in which the celebration of Sunday liturgy, where Catholics gather to celebrate the Eucharist, can maximize the potential for leading parishioners to deeper faith. "Each aspect of worship—the homily, the physical environment, hospitality, liturgical ministries, congregational participation, appropriate music, the Sunday bulletin with inclusions—has the potential to foster adult faith, bringing people into a more intimate relationship with Christ and with one another."[9]

Many of the ideas developed in the pastoral plan provide opportunities for lay initiatives and collaboration. On the other hand, it is important to remember in this context that the ministerial priesthood of the ordained has as its goal to build up the common priesthood of the baptized. In practical terms, that points to preaching that fully understands what the characteristic spiritual sacrifices of the laity in the parish are, and to the celebration of these actions of the faithful as the spiritual treasury of this community. When the parish gathers for Eucharist, it offers to the Father of Jesus these very real spiritual sacrifices along with the body of the Lord.

There are still too many parishes where the presiding priest and the other liturgical ministers communicate their fatigue and detachment through poorly prepared leadership, slipshod or vacuous preaching, and mechanical ritual actions. While life-giving celebrations nourish and deepen faith, poor celebrations can weaken and even destroy faith. Above all, we need the insight to establish a vital link between the Scriptures, the mystery of Christ, and the actual experiences of the parishioners. No other program or initiative in the church can possibly supplant the formative impact of Sunday celebrations.

Positively, however, life-giving preaching and liturgical leadership are immense graces for the faithful. Recently I observed a parish community respond with joy and appreciation during a Sunday Mass where everything was correct and some things were superb. During the preacher's wonderful homily, people around me smiled, nodded assent, and clearly took his words to heart. The priest's leadership in the Eucharistic Prayer was equally strong and touching. I was not too surprised at the end of Mass when a parishioner next to me said, "We are so lucky. Father Jack is a treasure." He is, and so are the many great priest-pastors who give their lives to building up the faithful in faith and service.

A second approach of the Bishops' Pastoral Plan for Adult Faith Formation describes family-centered activities for catechesis and faith formation. Here it says "There may be no place more significant for catechesis than the family."[10] The document notes that one of the major reasons people give for not coming to parish adult education meetings is that these events take them away from their families. So then the question becomes, how can we help couples and families believe that it is possible and important for them to grow in faith in their own homes?

A number of print vehicles are suggested: magazines, booklets, newsletters, etc. However, there are also "videos that promote family faith sharing [and] Catholic websites."[11] Much will depend on the social class, economic bracket, and ethnic culture of individual locales; but in some places, a coordinating website could prove to be a key to link the families of the parish to one another to offer them resources for faith learning. Many Catholics are spending more and more time in cyberspace. Evidently going there to meet them is an effective point of entry in getting their attention.

The third approach described is the development of small groups. A growing number of vital American parishes are developing various forms of small Christian communities to serve as the basic unit of the parish. Such communities can be based on neighborhood proximity, interest groups, ethnic links, or other rationales. However, whatever the basis for drawing the small community together, the smaller size allows for more personal and intense mutual interactions than those that are possible in the plenary parish assembly. The pastoral plan says: "Small communities are powerful vehicles for adult faith formation, providing opportunities for learning, prayer, mutual support, and the shared experience of Christian living and service to the church and society. Ecclesial movements and associations that are part of the vibrant life of the church make great contributions here."[12]

At several points in my own pastoral life, I have had the privilege of serving as chaplain or adviser to groups of lay couples. Returning from graduate studies in France, I was so impressed with the involvement of the French Dominicans with lay movements there that I wrote to the Christian Family Movement headquarters in Chicago to ask them to link me up as chaplain with a CFM group, if possible. They were happy to oblige, and thus began one of the best pastoral experiences of my priestly life.

There and also later in different places I found it true that these monthly meetings of couples for prayer, study, and friendship offered a form of social experience that was as rich for its privileged relationships as it was for its educational components. I could feel the joy and expectation of the couples as they began to gather, sharing stories of their children, their work, the parish, and their various avocations. That affective dynamic of spiritual friendship was at least as important in strengthening the faith of the participants as the explicit learning exercises. The "idea" of the Body of Christ, met so often in the Lectionary readings, took on features of friendship and intimacy through these small group relationships.

One thing that many Catholics miss in their lives today is what may be called "a Christian world." By that I mean a social context in which they feel at home in their Christian attitudes and values rather than like an endangered species. Such an atmosphere is a powerful component of such small Christian communities. In such a context, creative and competent adults dare to think imaginatively about a deeper involvement of their personal and family lives in spreading the kingdom of God, and how to take initiatives to render the parish more effective in its mission.

The fourth and fifth approaches in the bishops' document on adult faith formation are large group learning and individual activities. The former may include parish-based lectures, panel presentations and discussions, service projects, social events in the parish, and ecumenical activities, all of them including prayer and learning components.[13] Individual activities may be encouraged by a parish library or a shop for books, magazines, and audio and videotapes, as well as website informational pages and chat rooms that allow people to discuss their faith, find religious news and information, and also learn about prayer, the Catholic tradition, and Catholic social teaching.

Let me add that someone also needs to develop the potential for Christian teens to meet and mentor their peers through cyberspace. That is where many of them are to be found already. There's no better place to look for them with appropriate good news from the

Christian community. In some successful programs in parishes and schools, youth ministry begins with the Web. Although this resource presupposes a certain level of economic affluence, it is surprising how pervasive is the access of teens and young adults to the Internet. In any case, youth ministry cannot afford to forget the teens of the poor and the less well off and, naturally, Web-based ministries will be only one dimension of any youth ministry program.

An additional aspect of adult faith formation is growth in personal prayer. The bishops "encourage all Catholics to spend some time alone with God each day, whether they meditate on Scripture, use printed or memorized prayers, the Liturgy of the Hours, the rosary, meditation and contemplative prayer, or simply dwell in wordless praise in God's loving presence.[14] The role of prayer needs to be much more than a footnote here. The royal mission of the priesthood of the faithful and the source of their holiness is linked directly to the guiding force of the Holy Spirit. Mature prayer is precisely growing in attentiveness to the Spirit's action and learning ways of surrendering to God in silence and waiting. We will be saying more about personal prayer in the next chapter. The baptismal priesthood is exercised integrally through prayer.

This section of the bishops' Pastoral Plan for Adult Faith Formation concludes with a statement that has the potential to be revolutionary if bishops and priests in the U.S. take it seriously. Paragraph 112 says "Whatever approach is used, each parish needs to consider seriously how it will make the life-long faith formation of its adult members its chief catechetical concern." We could rephrase that sentence to say that helping the faithful of the parish to own the royal mission of their baptismal priesthood will require providing them with opportunities to network in study, prayer, and friendship with other couples, families, and individuals to learn, share, and serve. Is there any other priority for the Catholic Church in the U.S. more compelling than that?

HOLINESS IS NOT SELF-IMPROVEMENT

I fear that most Christians today, for some reason or other, imagine that they are supposed to get their act together on their own, and bring their good behavior to church with them on Sunday. Perhaps it has something to do with getting all dressed up for church as children. Who knows? However, for most of us there's not much good news in the idea that we are supposed to fix ourselves up on our own. That is not really the Gospel. The good news of the Gospel, flowing into the church's clear teaching about the priestly experience of the baptized, is that none of our individual struggles fall outside the scope of our participation in Christ's loving and redeeming self-sacrifice that we call his eternal priesthood.

The good news and the bad news of the Gospel is the same: "And the Word became flesh and lived among us, and we have seen his glory, the glory as of a father's only son, full of grace and truth" (John 1:14). The immense good news here is that God came and got right next to us in Jesus' incarnation. It is comforting to hear that we are loved, to learn that our sins have been forgiven, and to know that we have received the promise of everlasting life. Many baptized Christians find that "Good News" good enough to invest an hour in it every Sunday morning. The Good News sometimes grows stale, however, if we don't continually reflect upon it and invest our lives in it. But it is there—and it is good news. It gives us the reassurance that we have been called to eternal life.

The bad news is that unless this "Good News" becomes part of every day and every context, then it cannot be what it is meant to be for us, a transforming adoption of our lives into the living Christ. Most of us try to have it both ways—to be Sunday Christians with the comforts of a hopeful faith and to be weekday pagans with time off for bad behavior. Even serious Christians can feel themselves isolated and abandoned in the trials and struggles that are an inevitable part of the texture of their good lives. They have not fully understood the real significance of their Christian vocation and so can not apply the "Good News" to the bad news in their own lives.

From its earliest centuries, the church has pondered the mystery of Christ's role as a bridge. Not only is Christ in his humanity the bridge between everything human in us and his divinity, but he has crossed over that bridge to dwell inside our humanity. The Letter to the Hebrews, describing what Christ's priesthood means, says that "he had to become like his brothers and sisters in every respect, so that he might be a merciful and faithful high priest in the service of God, to make a sacrifice of atonement for the sins of the people" (Heb 2:17).

The consequence of this "likeness" to us "in every respect" is that Christ has reached out to be with us in our human condition. When we come up against a hedonistic culture, a mocking media, or calculating relationships, he is already there as grace and guide. He faced those same things in the circumstances of his life on earth, and he counts on us to face up to them in his name in our own circumstances. These challenges are not peripheral to our lives, but rather they are an integral part of our acceptance and living out of our redemption by Christ.

It is important to notice that part of the reason why today's faithful feel themselves in such a bind is that they get very little help from the culture. Print and media campaigns address them as needy and insecure consumers with pocketbooks; politicians' sound bites address them as self-interested hedonists with a seventh grade education; and the litigious society around them systematically grinds away at any remnant of a sense of the common good. When they watch television to relax, they too often find themselves confronted with soft pornography and mockery of traditional values. When they try to discuss the world with friends, they feel fearful of damaging their relationships if they betray any critical attitudes toward the new post-9/11 American patriotism.

Depending on their luck, they may or may not get better help from the church. In some places, most of the heavy trials of the faithful go largely untouched by the pastoral ministry of the ordained. There are other gospel values besides opposing the huge numbers of abortions in our country. When are they likely to hear the message that their renewed commitment to their marriage vows in the midst of weariness and relational conflicts is at the very heart of their participation in Christ's sacrificial love for them and for the church? How often does preaching link their hungers for meaning to their growth in spiritual maturity? Do Sunday celebration and preaching embrace them in their anxieties or distance them with the glib recitation of abstract ideals for a Christian life? Admittedly, it's no easier for their parish priests than it is for them to bring experience face to face with the grace of Christ. But never before has it been more important to try to do that. The family is the seedbed of the church's future.

One of the classic theological formulas of St. Thomas Aquinas for expressing the power of Christ in our life can be put roughly in this way: "Everything that Christ has assumed (taken to himself), he has redeemed."[15] Aquinas said that alienation and distance from God is the problem with human sinfulness, and that reconciliation through intimacy is the solution or "redemption" of those sinners. God's motive is not to exact punishment on those who have failed or disobeyed, but to befriend those who have not yet understood the reality of divine love.

Instead of being distanced from Christ by our psychological, moral, or social struggles, we must learn to recognize them as opportunities to embrace the redeeming power of the Savior. He saves us by showing us how to be strong under attack, faithful despite temptations, and patient and generous when we are annoyed by those whom we love. When we follow his example, we are not merely "being good," we are participating in Christ's victory over sin.

Earlier in chapter 4, we made an important distinction between what we called the "graced sign" and the "realized mystery." In the Eucharist, the graced sign is the transubstantiated bread and wine that actually brings onto the altar the presence of Christ as transforming food, and then brings him into the lives of those who receive him. The graced sign has as its goal and meaning to bring about the realized mystery, which in this case is the transformed life of the communicants, who become a living sacrament of Christ's presence. In this way, Christ comes to be present in our relationships, in our families and homes, in our workplace, and in all the circumstances of our lives. Since through their participation in the Eucharist, the laity have become the "realized mystery" of the Body of Christ, Vatican II describes the life of couples and families as "the domestic church."[16]

The Council's decree on the laity expresses this teaching in a vivid manner: "The mission of being the primary vital cell of society has been given to the family by God. This mission will be accomplished if the family, by the mutual affection of its members and by family prayer, presents itself as a domestic sanctuary of the church; if the whole family takes its part in the church's liturgical worship; if, finally, it offers active hospitality, and practices justice and other good works for the benefit of all its sisters and brothers who suffer from want. . . . Christian families bear a very valuable witness to Christ before the world when all their life they remain attached to the Gospel and give clear examples of Christian marriage."[17]

The whole agenda of the "domestic church"—including the faithful journey of the couple toward life-giving intimacy, their care for and instruction of their children, their relationships with those near and far (including extended family and workplace colleagues)—this whole agenda is graced. Christ's plan is that these relationships and interactions will draw upon the grace of the sacraments of baptism, confirmation, and matrimony, as well as, of course, the Eucharist.

Going back to our previous remarks about sacraments, we know that the sacramentality of the domestic church means two things. On the one hand, the grace of these sacraments is the action of the Holy Spirit upon the persons, relationships, and actions of those involved. On the other hand, the fruit of this spiritual gift is the enhancement of Christ's presence to the couple, to the family, and through them to the society surrounding them. Christ becomes the reconciling and affirming presence in which friends and family meet in faith and in the Holy Spirit. This gift of reconciliation and vocation shapes the quality of these persons' lives, giving them a vitality and luminosity that are at the core of their Christian witness as disciples.

The sacraments create the conditions for the anointing-empowering action of the Spirit in the lives of believers. The result of that guidance and inspiration of the Holy Spirit is what we called in the last chapter a prophetic presence and what we recognize here as the reign of God or God's ruling power in our lives in the context of our daily responsibilities, hardships, and joys. The royal mission of the priesthood of the faithful is essentially to prepare themselves to be led by the Spirit's guidance.

This is where lay Christians are meant to find their holiness. Holiness is not about our impressing God, but about God embracing us. When the Council speaks of holiness, it describes it in terms of determined commitment to exercising the talents and responsibilities of each life in a spirit of faith. "The forms and tasks of life are many but there is one holiness, which is cultivated by all who are led by God's Spirit and, obeying the Father's voice and adoring God the Father in spirit and in truth, follow Christ, poor and humble in carrying his cross, that they may deserve to be sharers in his glory. All, however, according to their own gifts and duties must steadfastly advance along the way of a living faith, which arouses hope and works through love."[18] It is the whole of creation and the whole social world that is the object of this transformation. If only those who live and work in its midst understood the power of the grace that is offered them! The language of the Council here is too stiff and churchy. What it really means is that all of us will find our holiness on our doorstep.

Thomas Merton pointed out half a century ago that many people fail to become saints because they imagine that holiness means imitating the lives and behavior of others whose circumstances are utterly alien to their own.[19] But in fact holiness means first of all "realness," becoming that irreplaceable person whose gifts and presence are unrepeatable. Parallel to the expression in John's Gospel cited above, we have to say here that not only is the eternal Word of God—God's Son—a word becoming flesh and living in our midst, but also each one of us is a *word* that God wills to express in the unfolding stories of our lives. Married or single, young or old, intellectual or down to earth, professional or service worker—whatever the circumstances of life, each person is a *word* in the divine plan of redeeming love. Each one is invited to be a dynamic and expressive member of the Body of Christ.

As we have noted in the chapter on baptism, this vocation to sacramental significance in the Body of Christ carries with it a bias toward communal as opposed to individualistic expression. That is why relationships are so important in the Christian sacramental life and also why the relation of the partners in the sacrament of matrimony is a sign of grace. The family is the foundation for the social reality of the church and, as such, it is blessed. This sacred character of the Christian family does not preclude the family's immersion in the untidy give and take of personal adjustments and developmental struggles. All of that is the symbolic matter for the graced sign of the couple (and the family as a whole) courageously committing themselves to one another for the sake of (and *as*) the Body of Christ. In parallel fashion, the relationships, friendships, commitments, work, and service of single Christians in the parish and civic community form the symbolic matter for their graced sign as members of Christ.

The story of Jesus Christ's own incarnation narrative is evidence enough of the fact that when God acts in human history, God's grace works not with some theoretically ideal set of circumstances, but rather with the available reality of the world. The savior of humankind, God's own Son, was born on a family trip, in a borrowed stable. His life was threatened by a lunatic king. He grew up in a most unpromising rustic setting. Whatever else could these details of Luke's Gospel story mean for us, except that our own life circumstances, however unlikely they may appear to our eyes, are perfectly apt for inclusion in the continuing story of Christ's Body on earth?

The focal point for Christian holiness is not moral self-improvement. The strange truth is that sometimes only a fall into some trouble or mischief will wake people up to realize that they are unable to take care of themselves or keep up a front of moral rectitude. God's agenda is transformation through intimacy, not moral self-improvement for respectability. Some very earnest Christians truly seeking to grow in holiness live behind prison bars, having discovered their vocation to holiness after a fall. We should not forget that John the Baptist and the apostles Peter and Paul were imprisoned at some point in their lives. Jesus emphasizes our finding him in the imprisoned and visiting "him" in that context (Matt 25:36, 43-4). The Gospel is not patient with any false respectability.

The agenda for Christian holiness in fact is the ruling force of the Holy Spirit within us. This is the social meaning of the kingdom of God. God's kingdom is a community of individuals who seek together to grow into a unity at the service of God's guiding Spirit and to become docile to the Spirit's inspirations. Becoming responsive to that inspiration of the Holy Spirit is exactly what we mean by holiness. Whether as families or parish communities, we do not sufficiently realize the significance of the sign value of our Christian solidarity. The "domestic church" is itself a sacrament which is all the more telling in its impact when it is rooted in the heart of human society—in neighborhoods and in immediate proximity to the attitudes and values of our friends and companions.

A RENEWED VISION OF FAITHFULNESS

Encouraged by another couple who are close friends, Bob and Janet attended a renewal program in their parish church that offered four weekly evening sessions of prayer and preaching. The visiting preacher devoted his talks to the priesthood of the baptized and the domestic church. Following these four evenings, Bob and Janet agreed to participate for some months in follow-up meetings along with four other couples from the parish in order to explore the theology they learned as it applies to their own experience. The honest sharing among these couples has been a revelation of "ordinary holiness." The ideas they received are taking root.

At the parish renewal sessions, Bob heard and recognized the meaning of his marriage and family responsibilities as a vocation, a call from God. That means that these relationships, with all their trials and joys, are God's will for him. This new understanding somehow brings Bob a feeling of peace and joy. He still experiences restless moments and sometimes imagines more exciting ways to work and live. But he now sees the significance of his family life as a vocation. That has become a help, a gift of light and direction that is more authoritative than his unpredictable and distracting whims. God's will is God's ruling power in his life, and his obedience is his share in his Lord's royal mission.

Janet found their renewal program helpful too. She took away an awareness of her profound link to the suffering and strength of the Lord in her patient nurturing of her own growing children and of her students as well. She recognizes echoes of Christ's vulnerabilities in her own. She can see how openness to Bob and to her children, her patience and fidelity, are a real means of life and support for them. Janet understands that it is precisely this family context, one that requires so much generosity and so many seemingly unrequited initiatives from her, which is the source of her holiness. To be faithful as Christ is faithful is to live according to his Spirit.

Maria had the good fortune to be introduced to a small Christian community that is made up of members of several parishes. Several other participants in this group are also Latino, and she is finding relief and strength in having their support and friendship. Maria still loves and misses her dead husband, Juan. But with the help of her little community she feels more in communion with him in her love and prayer across the abyss created by his death. She is no longer alone in her struggle.

Maria has learned how to focus her determination and generosity with "little prayers": "Lord, let me care and give love without resentment, just as you did"; "Lord, be the love in my love and the love in my heart." Frankly, Maria has a lot more joy and gratitude in her heart these days, even though very little of substance has changed in the outward circumstances of her life.

All these earnest Christians are more contented with their lives and feel more alive and expectant. Something new has come into their experience. Might it be the kingdom of God?

Notes

1. The phrase, "Love persons, use things; not vice versa," is lifted from a writing of Ruel Howe entitled *Human Need and God's Action*. It is noteworthy that Immanuel Kant spoke of the domain of moral philosophy treating of the relations of persons one to another as "the kingdom of ends."

2. John Paul II, "The Lay Members of Christ's Faithful People" *(Christifideles Laici)*, n. 14.

3. See, e.g., *Summa Theologiae*, II II, 81, 7.

4. This theme is clearly and helpfully developed in G. Emery, "Le sacerdoce spirituel des fidèles chez saint Thomas d'Aquin," *Revue Thomiste* 99:4 (Jan.–Mar. 1999) 211–43.

5. *Christifideles Laici*, n. 14.

6. Some excellent recent studies that bear on this idea are these: Vincent J. Miller, *Consuming Religion: Christian Faith and Practice in a Consumer Society* (New York: Continuum, 2004); Quentin Schultze, *Communicating for Life: Christian Stewardship in Community and Media* (Grand Rapids: Baker Academic Books, 2000); and Richard R. Gaillardetz, *Transforming Our Days: Spirituality, Community, and Liturgy in a Technological Culture* (New York: Crossroad, 2000).

7. Decree on the Apostolate of Lay People, n. 11.

8. *Our Hearts Were Burning Within Us: A Pastoral Plan for Adult Faith Formation in the United States* (Washington, DC: United States Catholic Conference, 1999) §97.

9. Ibid., §101.

10. Ibid., §102.

11. Ibid., §104.

12. Ibid., §106.

13. Ibid., §107.

14. Ibid., §109–10.

15. See *Summa Theologiae* III, 31, 1; 31, 2; and 31, 7 ad 3. M.-D. Chenu glosses these texts with the following graphic explanation: "Divine life assumes, without any waste, the whole of human life. The incarnation continues in the mystical body of Christ. Work, business, companies, professions, factories, offices: nothing can be a stranger to the Christian life. The whole of human civilization is the terrain of Christianity." This text appears in M.-D. Chenu, *La Parole de Dieu II: L'Evangile dans le temps* (Paris: Cerf, 1964) 97 (my translation).

16. Dogmatic Constitution on the Church, n. 11

17. Decree on the Apostolate of Lay People, n. 11.

18. Dogmatic Constitution on the Church, n. 41.

19. Thomas Merton, *New Seeds of Contemplation* (New York: New Directions, 1961) 98.

Chapter 7

Lives Lifted in Praise

Years ago I taught for a semester in India. Thanks to the hospitality of some Jesuit friends, I also spent a week in the neighboring Himalayan kingdom of Nepal before returning to North America. Those were mysterious, memorable days.

On a sunny morning in December, I visited a mountain shrine in the hills outside Kathmandu. That particular day was the feast of the Hindu goddess Kali, and devotees were approaching the forest shrine bringing animals to be sacrificed at the temple to seek the favor of the goddess. We parked our van about a mile away from the temple and our group walked slowly uphill along a path that paralleled a fast-running stream. Before we reached the temple, the stream's water ran red with blood.

On the way before us were pilgrims carrying lambs, goats, chickens, and other birds. In silence, the slow-moving procession mounted a wooded hill and then suddenly descended into a sanctuary spread across a natural amphitheater surrounded by great boulders. There the stream descended from above in a splashing cascade.

Near the falling water was a stone altar and just beyond it a typical Indian pagoda-like temple sheltering a marble statue of Kali. There the people brought flowers, burning lamps, and rice offerings. Next to the altar stood a burly priest dressed in white cotton spattered with blood. He received the animals to be sacrificed to the goddess. With swift, economical movements he lifted up a goat by the head, slit its throat as it squealed a blood-curdling cry of desperation, poured out its blood on the altar, and then proceeded to take part of the carcass for himself and return part to the owner of the animal. The goat's blood ran down the altar and then into the stream. The entire act of sacrifice took just minutes. It was a silent tryst between the devotee and the god.

This outpouring of blood went on through the morning as a continuing file of worshipers climbed up to the temple. I wondered about the priests' training (there were two of them, and they took turns helping the people). Weightlifting must be a mandatory course in whatever seminary prepared them for this ritual performance. Many of the animals were clearly heavy, and subduing their jerking, frenetic movements required great physical strength. Beyond that, there was something compelling about the poise and sobriety of the priests while they were engaged in the systematic work of ritual death and blood-letting. It was evident that they felt themselves caught up in a sacred duty.

For years before that, I had read with fascination about ancient temple sacrifices, both in the Old Testament and in studies of the ancient religions of the Near East. But blood in the pages of a book is very different from blood spurting from the gashed open neck of a writhing beast. Here in the hills outside Kathmandu I found a ritual as ancient as recorded human history. I was watching the enactment of an instinct deep in the human heart—the hunger to appease, influence, and enchant divine power through fierce acts of animal sacrifice.

Much of Old Testament history is a narrative about the Hebrews slipping into the customs of the people around them while the prophets rail against their idolatry. The Hebrew prophets warned against the "high places" of the Canaanites, where altars were built to sacrifice to the Baals (the local gods of the pagans surrounding the Hebrews in their promised land). For example, in Jeremiah 32:35, we see the prophet's warning against human sacrifice: "They built the high places of Baal in the valley of the son of Hinnom, to offer up their sons and daughters to Molech [a Canaanite deity], though I did not command them, nor did it enter my mind that they should do this abomination, causing Judah to sin."

In the periods which archaeologists refer to as the Early (1250–1000 B.C.E.) and Middle (900–600 B.C.E.) Iron Age, Near Eastern people worshiped a plurality of gods whose influence was imagined to be territorial. So even after the Lord God led the Hebrews from slavery in Egypt to a new life in the land of Canaan, they were constantly tempted to worship the local gods at the hilltop shrines they found there. These "high places" surely had been ancient sanctuaries long before the Hebrews arrived on the scene.

Occasional passages of the Old Testament lay bare arcane stories of idolatry that cause one to shudder at the violence sometimes linked to ancient religions. A strange and poignant story from the Book of Judges tells of Jephthah, who made this vow to the Lord as he strove to subdue the troublesome Ammonites: "If you will give the Ammonites into my hand, then whoever comes out of the doors of my house to meet me, when I return victorious from the Ammonites, shall be the Lord's, to be offered up by me as a burnt offering." Jephthah then proceeded to fight against the Ammonites, "and the Lord gave them into his hand" (Judg 11:30-32).

When Jephthah came home, "there was his daughter coming out to meet him with timbrels and with dancing. She was his only child; he had no son or daughter except her" (11:34). His poor daughter, once she understood her bad luck, asked her father's leave "to go and wander on the mountains" for two months to mourn her fate. After her ritual murder, "there arose an Israelite custom that for four days every year the daughters of Israel would go out to lament the daughter of Jephthah" (Judg 11:40).

Jephthah considered his vow irrevocable and he followed through on it. Jephthah, a judge in Israel, was a faithful believer in the Lord. But this story shows how he also shared the ideas of his environment. Even though Leviticus (18:21) forbids human sacrifice, that violent custom had penetrated the imagination of the Hebrew people under the influence of their Canaanite neighbors. This tragic story gives some inkling of the theology at work behind blood offerings.

THE RITUAL OF BLOOD SACRIFICE

Sacrifice means anything offered to God to appease the anger of the deity or to atone for sin. Sacrifices tend to be both impressive and drastic, especially at times of festival or in times of crisis. This is how the offering of the life of a living creature fits into the picture.

In ritual sacrifices, blood is the essential element. Blood is the most powerful physical symbol of life and death. Blood is the gift from God that sustains life in living beings. In the visceral logic of the ancient ritual world, the blood of any living being is a divine substance. Only God can make something alive; and only blood sustains the life of the living. Consequently the blood of any living being was considered to be an agent of divine purification and a shield against ritual impurity (cf. Lev 17:11). To pour out a living creature's blood in sacrifice is to offer back to God the most mysterious and precious gift that a human being can touch. To offer the blood of something or someone dear is to multiply the personal significance of the gift.

Priests poured blood upon the altar of the Temple and all around it (Lev 1:5; 9:12). In the book of Exodus, the ritual for the night of Passover instructs the Hebrews to mark their lintels with blood (12:7) to preserve their houses from the destroying angel. Moreover, in the ritual of expiation, the blood of the sacrificed animals is sprinkled on the people. In a similar way, the blood of sacrifice is smeared upon priests in their rite of consecration (Exod 29:20; Lev 8:23, 30).

Besides blood-letting, all these rituals have an additional dynamic in common. They are initiatives that human beings undertake to gain the attention and favor of the divine. These rites give people a feeling that there is something they can do to control a dicey situation, such as Jephthah's rash promise to God before he went to battle against the Ammonites. The illusion of control supplied by the ritual provides supplicants with reassurance in times of risk and fear. What could be more graphic than a sanctuary dripping in blood?

We need to remember that this system of bloody temple sacrifices was still in place during Jesus' lifetime. Chapter 2 of Luke's Gospel shows the parents of Jesus offering a purification sacrifice for their infant son in the temple at Jerusalem. They offered "turtle doves or . . . pigeons," because they were too poor to afford a sheep (cf. Lev 12:18). Yet, as pious Jews, despite their poverty, Mary and Joseph felt themselves obliged to perform the purification ritual for Jesus.

JESUS' PHYSICAL AND SPIRITUAL SACRIFICE

John's Gospel makes the blood of Jesus a central element of his account of the passion and its interpretation. In John 19:34, the soldier who came to verify that Jesus had indeed died on the cross "pierced his side with a spear, and at once blood and water came out." In John's symbolic description, this scene links the death of the Lord to the sacraments of baptism and Eucharist. The water is a sign of the Spirit's transforming action in the water of baptism: "Very truly, I tell you, no one can enter the kingdom of God without being born of water and Spirit. What is born of the flesh is flesh, and what is born of the Spirit is spirit" (John 3:5-6). Further, the blood of Christ's sacrifice is shared with his disciples at the eucharistic table: "Those who eat my flesh and drink my blood have eternal life, and I will raise them up on the last day. . . . Those who eat my flesh and drink my blood abide in me, and I in them" (John 6:54, 56).

First Corinthians (1 Cor 11:25) and the Synoptic Gospels (Mark, Matthew, and Luke) called the eucharistic blood of Christ the sign of a new covenant. So in Luke (22:20) we read "This cup that is poured out for you is the new covenant in my blood." To grasp the significance of this imagery, we need to look to the Old Testament antecedent.

The old covenant at Sinai is described in Exodus with striking detail: "Then [Moses] took the book of the covenant, and read it in the hearing of the people; and they said, 'All that the Lord has spoken we will do, and we will be obedient.' Moses took the blood and dashed it on the people, and said, 'See the blood of the covenant that the Lord has made with you in accordance with all these words'" (Exod 24:7-8).

It is critical to notice in these descriptions of Old Testament religion that the offerings are material beings whose life and blood are symbolic of the lives of the worshipers, but not organically connected to them. While such sacrifices might be offered with great piety and deep personal investment, they might also become mere formalities. Without careful attention, ritual is just ritual and the heartfelt link to the divine can be lost in the manipulation of the elements. That such a disappointing outcome was at least sometimes the case, is clear from the following texts:

> I [God] hate, I despise your festivals, and take no delight in your solemn assemblies. Even though you offer me your burnt offerings and grain offerings, I will not accept them. . . . But let justice roll down like water, and righteousness like an ever-flowing stream. (Amos 5:21, 24)
>
> For you [God] have no delight in sacrifice; if I were to give a burnt offering, you would not be pleased. The sacrifice acceptable to God is a broken spirit; a broken and contrite heart, O God, you will not despise. (Ps 51:16)

In these texts, God is displeased because the people have allowed their acts of sacrifice to become merely externalized, material acts that do not arise from their own loving hearts. After all, as Psalm 50 explains, these sacrifices are not required to feed the deity: "For every wild animal of the forest is mine [says God], the cattle on a thousand hills. . . Do I eat the flesh of bulls, or drink the blood of goats?" (Ps 50:10-13).

Their only purpose is to symbolize and express love and thanksgiving to God for God's constant and faithful help.

Returning to the New Testament, we see the clearest expression of the change from bloody to unbloody sacrifice in the Letter to the Hebrews. The sacred writer tells us that according to the Law the same sacrifices are continually offered again and again, "But in these sacrifices there is a reminder of sin year after year. For it is impossible for the blood of bulls and goats to take away sins" (10:3-4). Christ's sacrifice, on the other hand, was once and for all: "But when Christ had offered for all time a single sacrifice for sins, 'He sat down at the right hand of God,' and since then has been waiting 'until his enemies would be made a footstool for his feet.' For by a single offering he has perfected for all time those who are sanctified" (10:12-14).

Moreover, Christ abolishes the old covenant of bloody sacrifice and burnt offerings and establishes a new covenant: "Christ . . . entered once for all into the Holy Place, not with the blood of goats and calves, but with his own blood, thus obtaining eternal redemption. . . . (9:11) For this reason he is the mediator of a new covenant, so that those who are called may receive the promised eternal inheritance. . . . (9:15) For Christ did not enter a sanctuary made by human hands, a mere copy of the true one, but he entered into heaven itself, now to appear in the presence of God on our behalf" (9:24).

Christ's sacrifice puts an end to the age-old system of ritual blood-letting. His gift to God the Father is the gift of his own life.

THE SACRIFICE OF A NEW CREATION

The mystery of Jesus' incarnation is the beginning of a new creation. Jesus Christ is, as St. Paul calls him, "the firstborn within a large family" of those "predestined to be conformed to the image of [the] Son" (Rom 8:30, 29). When Christ inaugurated the new covenant or system of sacrifice that replaced the immolation of another victim with his own self-sacrifice, he removed the possibility that his disciples might offer substitution sacrifices in the Temple as a path to sanctification. Rather, Christ draws his disciples, through their participation in the eucharistic sacrifice, into his own victory over sin and death. As St. Paul described this in 1 Cor 10:16f. "The cup of blessing that we bless, is it not a sharing in the blood of Christ? The bread that we break, is it not a sharing in the body of Christ? Because there is one bread, we who are many are one body, for we all partake of the one bread." In the Eucharist, we give ourselves to the Body of Christ and join our sacrifices to the one effective sacrifice that is Christ's. In chapter 4, we spoke of the meaning of "spiritual sacrifices." They are our participation in Christ's eternally valid self-offering as the one holocaust entirely pleasing to God. We—as *many* who are yet *one* in his Spirit, and as members of his body—link our own inner self-sacrifice to Christ's. This is the meaning of our baptismal priesthood.

No longer will that ancient human hunger to rattle the gates of heaven with stupendous acts of bloody sacrifice be channeled into the spilling of blood. No longer will the spattering of the blood and the offering of slaughtered beasts be our ritual path to sanctification. It is not the blood of bulls or sheep that can purify us, but our own blood, sweat, and tears made one with the Blood of Christ. That is our path to salvation.

We are redeemed by the self-offering of God's divine Son, a holocaust of love and compassion that redeems us by embracing the very poverty of our condition. Christ does not offer something other than himself, and we do not offer something other than ourselves. We are joined to him as members of his Mystical Body. Our suffering, pain, hope, and love are gathered into Christ's self-sacrifice and are ennobled by it. His humanity becomes the bridge by which we cross over from the futility of temple offerings to the saving mystery of our salvation.

THE OFFERING

During the Mass, the priest gathers the prayers of the faithful and presents them to God. The priestly mission of the baptismal priesthood gathers together the spiritual treasures of our lives to offer them as a work of thanksgiving to the Divine Reality who is our origin and our foundation. This is the sacrifice that God desires from us. God's plea throughout the biblical history of salvation has always been for a people entirely his own, whose lives and hearts become the witness from which the world may read God's message of truth and goodness. That is still God's dream for humanity.

Christ's disciples are called to devoted self-oblation in gratitude and compassion. The apostolic letters of the New Testament elaborate various ways of spelling out this vocation:

> I appeal to you therefore, brothers and sisters, by the mercies of God, to *present your bodies as a living sacrifice*, holy and acceptable to God, which is your spiritual worship. (Rom 12:1)

Let the word of Christ dwell in you richly; teach and admonish one another in all wisdom; and with gratitude in your hearts sing psalms, hymns, and spiritual songs to God. And whatever you do, in word or deed, *do everything in the name of the Lord Jesus*, giving thanks to God the Father through him. (Col 3:16)

[L]ike living stones, let yourselves be built into a spiritual house, to be a holy priesthood, *to offer spiritual sacrifices acceptable to God* through Jesus Christ. (1 Pet 2:5)

The letter to the Romans exhorts us to present our bodies as a sacrifice; Colossians urges us to do whatever we do, in word or deed, in the name of the Lord Jesus; and 1 Peter instructs us to turn our lives into spiritual sacrifices. The stuff of life is the matter of this priestly action of those joined to Christ the high priest through their baptism. How do we manage to do this? One of the most important observances for the priestly life of the baptized is to offer intentionally the actions and experiences of each day to God as a sacrifice of praise.

In a capitalistic culture that strives relentlessly to intrude upon the springs of desire and human interest by stimulating artificial hungers for consumer goods, the pursuit of a fully conscious intentional life is a counter cultural (if not heroic) stance. A recent article in the *New York Times Magazine* crowed brightly about the achievements of cognitive psychology applied to advertising, claiming that we are arriving at a historic new moment in which advertisers will be able to scientifically stimulate consumers' desires for products. Instead of issuing a warning to readers about their potential dehumanization, the article presented its news as another breakthrough for the scientific world. The absence of a spiritual life was simply taken for granted by the author and the researchers on whose work he reported.[1]

By contrast, biblical religion has always insisted upon intention. Put in other words, the Bible resolutely reminds human beings that there is an "inside" to their actions, a "heart" that guides their decisions. As Luke 6 puts it, "The good person out of the good treasure of the heart produces good, and the evil person out of evil treasure produces evil; for it is out of the abundance of the heart that the mouth speaks" (Luke 6:45).

To talk about intentionality is ultimately to insist upon our divine destiny. To talk about what we "intend" is to name the goal or end toward which our lives are directed. Biblical revelation shows us that God is both our beginning and our end, our "Alpha and Omega." So intentionality means keeping that destiny clear and conscious; it means roughly the same thing as mindfulness. Consequently, intentionality provides a comprehensive significance to the whole of life.

Catholics who attended Catholic schools before the Second Vatican Council (and many who are younger) were taught a prayer that was called "The Morning Offering." As a child in a parochial grade school I recited this prayer along with the other pupils under the solemn supervision of my homeroom sister each morning. It became ingrained as a part of my Catholic consciousness.

The Morning Offering addresses itself to God the Father, asking that God will receive as a sacrifice of love all the thoughts, desires, and actions that I will perform throughout the day, joining them to the sacrifice of Christ through the mystery of the Eucharist. Here is one example of a formula for the Morning Offering:

> Source of all being, loving God, I offer you my life this day through Christ in the power of the Holy Spirit. Receive all my prayers, works, joys, and sufferings in union with the dying and rising of my Savior. Grant me patience, joy and understanding until the day that you call me to yourself. Glory to you, God, Father, Son, and Holy Spirit.[2]

I found another similar formula pasted in the front of my mother's Bible after her death. It reads as follows:

> O God, early in the morning I cry to you. Help me to pray and to concentrate my thoughts on you. I know that I cannot do this alone, for in me there is darkness, but with you there is light. I am lonely, but you do not leave me. I am feeble in heart, but with you there is help. I am restless, but with you there is peace. In me there is bitterness, but with you there is patience. I do not understand your way for me. Restore me to liberty, and enable me to live now, that I may answer before you and before me. And whatever this day may bring, your name be praised.

So many of the individual actions of busy people, especially the domestic preoccupations of mothers of young children, can become scattered or lost in a fog of preoccupations. Quite literally, the desire of the Morning Offering is to subsume all these moments into an intentional and conscious unity as spiritual sacrifices in the sense of which we have spoken. Changing diapers, preparing meals, cleaning house, picking up after children, working late, listening to the painful needs of friends—all these can seem like time wasted, unless they are bound together into the unity of a spiritual life aiming at solidarity with Christ's loving sacrifice.

We get some sense of the theology behind this prayer of intentionality by looking at the offertory rite in the Mass. The Offertory Prayer speaks as follows: "Blessed are you, Lord God of all creation; through your goodness we have this bread and wine to offer: fruit of the earth, work of human hands, they will become for us our spiritual food and drink."

In parallel fashion, just as the bread and wine, which are the "symbolic matter" of the rite of Eucharist, become a "graced sign"—the Body and Blood of the Lord—leading us to the "realized mystery" of the mystical body; so also the joys and sacrifices of our daily experience are "symbolic matter." Why not treat them in a similar way? Why not pray that, in union with Christ's sacrifice to which we join ourselves in the Eucharist, our daily actions may become our contribution to the "realized mystery" of the body of Christ? It seems obvious to me that we should pray as follows:

> Blessed are you, Lord God of compassion; through your Providence we have this time of frustration and patience to offer: may it become for us our share in the mystery of Christ's death and resurrection. . . .
>
> Blessed are you, Lord God of the universe; through your goodness we have the work of this day to offer, fruit of our concentration and our hopeful perseverance; may it become for us a channel of your Spirit's power and a worthy oblation of praise to your glory. . . .
>
> Blessed are you, Lord God of peace; through your goodness we have this family life together to offer: times of conflict and times of mercy; may it become for us a communion in your divine exchange of life and love. . . .

Here we behold the "realized mystery" of the Eucharist. Its fruition in our daily acts, united in love with Christ's self-offering to his Father, embraces the whole scope of our ordinary lives. A text that we have already examined, the Dogmatic Constitution on the Church of Vatican II (n. 34), expresses the Catholic theological tradition that the baptized join their lives in their most concrete details to Christ's redeeming sacrifice:

For all their works, if accomplished in the Spirit, become spiritual sacrifices acceptable to God through Jesus Christ: their prayers and apostolic undertakings, family and married life, daily work, relaxation of mind and body, even the hardships of life if patiently borne. . . . In the celebration of the Eucharist, these are offered to the Father in all piety along with the body of the Lord.

LINKING THE ORDINARY TO THE ETERNAL MYSTERY

One of my deepest motivations for writing this book is my recognition that so many Christians interpret their suffering and frustration as distractions from and impediments to their sanctification, instead of a means of sacramental union with Christ. Of course, it is the nature of suffering to weary our bodies and cloud our perception. Yet Christ took our troubled condition upon himself so as to link our pain and mortality to his and make them instruments that can lead us to the grace of redeemed life.

The Christian spiritual tradition has always realized that our suffering can be linked to Christ's redemptive gift through faith and intentionality. We should desire and intend to make our sacrifices, however concrete and ordinary, one with the sacrifice of Christ. In fact, our actions and our sufferings can provide the "exterior" dimension of our prayer just as well as words. We don't always have to *say* a prayer; we can *live out* a prayer. This is how "ceaseless prayer" comes to be achieved in the Christian life.

In classical Catholic theology, the word *intend* has the strong sense of providing an orientation or destination for our moral actions. By expressing through our Morning Offering our intention to offer all our works, prayers, thoughts, and desires, we orient the meaning of our lives and actions toward the love and service of God. So strong is this intentional orientation, that it has been understood by Catholic theology to provide light and direction even when actions carry our attention away from conscious prayer to the immediate needs of our duties. In other words, the affection of our heart is more important than the attention of our mind in binding our individual actions to the service of God.

St. Thomas Aquinas offers a helpful teaching to explain this idea in his *Summa Theologiae*:

Three kinds of attention are possible in prayer. One kind attends to the words, lest one err in pronouncing them, a second attends to the sense of the words, and a third attends to the end of the prayer, namely to God, and to the thing for which we are praying. This last kind of attention is most necessary. . . . Moreover, this attention whereby the mind is fixed upon God is sometimes so strong that the mind forgets all other things. . . .[3]

About this third kind of attention, we might say that the *heart attends* to the reality and presence of God even when words and conscious ideas lapse into the background.

We can gain further insight into Aquinas' understanding about prayer and intention from a similar text, in which he writes that ". . . in individual prayer, words and signs should be used insofar as they help to arouse the mind internally. If these signs impede or distract the mind, as often happens in those whose mind is sufficiently prepared for devotion without such signs, they should [no longer] be used."[4]

To paraphrase these texts of Aquinas, not only words but also loving actions and patient suffering can provide the visible and external dimension of Christian prayer. When a person's intention to serve God and grow in intimacy with God is rooted in the heart's movement toward God, then that affective dimension becomes the principal aspect of the life of prayer. In the course of a long and busy day, what will be most important is to renew repeatedly the intention of serving God and responding with grateful love to God's gifts.

One way of periodically reorienting our intention of offering our life in sacrifice to God is an ancient Christian tradition of repeated "little prayers." This tradition developed in the early church due to the fascination of the monks in the Egyptian desert and the early Western monasteries with St. Paul's exhortation in I Thessalonians to pray always: "Rejoice always, pray without ceasing, give thanks in all circumstances; for this is the will of God in Christ Jesus for you. Do not quench the Spirit" (1 Thess 5:16-19).

This passage from Thessalonians became one of the formative texts for early Christian monasticism. The goal of the fathers and mothers of the desert became ceaseless prayer and, with that, "imageless" prayer. The two things were linked in much the same way that Aquinas would later link them (as in the texts of his that we just examined). "Imageless" prayer is a movement of a person's mind and heart toward union with God based on faith and love in which the heart's strong desire and gratitude become the focus of attention. Although imageless prayer builds upon all our previous external prayer, study, practice, and thought, it results from God calling us beyond images into an exchange of mutual endearment. Imageless prayer is the simplification of prayer into its kernel—its essence—which is grateful love.

God is invisible but present to us in his gifts, especially the gift of our own life. Yet, despite the ever-present gift of God to us, we cannot hope to see God except in the "sacraments" of his created effects. When we recognize these gifts, we are moved to offer thanks and enter into a conscious relationship with God. So the goal of our prayer is to reach out with love through our heart's constant movement toward God.

Around the turn of the fifth century, the great monastic teacher, John Cassian, who had lived among the Egyptian desert monks, wrote about their monastic practices in his *Conferences*[5] and *Institutes*.[6] He is one of our chief windows into the spiritual life of the desert monks. In his tenth conference, Cassian writes as follows about the nature of ceaseless prayer:

> This will be the case when every love, every desire, every effort, every undertaking, every thought of ours, everything that we live, that we speak, that we breathe, will be God, and when that unity which the Father now has with the Son and which the Son has with the Father will be carried over into our understanding and our mind, so that, just as he loves us with a sincere and pure and indissoluble love, we too may be joined to him with a perpetual and inseparable love and so united with him that whatever we breathe, whatever we understand, whatever we speak, may be God.[7]

The scope and concreteness of Cassian's description of ceaseless prayer resembles that of the Council's Constitution on the Church (n. 34) that we quoted above. Although Cassian does not explicitly call these actions of the disciples "spiritual sacrifices," we can see that he clearly means the same thing. Achieving the intention of union with the Father in the Son through the Holy Spirit is exactly the point of "ceaseless prayer." It touches everything that we do.

How can we bring about this great elevation of our lives into ceaseless union with Christ through constant prayer? Cassian tells us about the teaching of Abba Isaac, one of the great masters of the Egyptian desert. Isaac taught Cassian that someone seeking a life of constant prayer should repeat a brief formula that so fills the mind with awareness of God that all other thoughts are driven out. Cassian explains Isaac's instruction as follows:

> Every monk who longs for the continual awareness of God should be in the habit of meditating on [this formula] ceaselessly in his heart, after having driven out every kind of thought, because he will be unable to hold fast to it in any other way than by being freed from all bodily cares and concerns. . . . This, then, is the devotional formula proposed to you as absolutely necessary for possessing the perpetual awareness of God: "O God, incline unto my aid; O Lord, make haste to help me."[8]

(The Scripture quotes are the first two phrases of Psalm 70, now used universally in the Western church to introduce the hours of the divine office.)

The dust of the wilderness trails and the burning heat of the African desert still cling to Cassian's narrative. Reading his account about the teachings of Abba Isaac, we need to imagine the spiritual hunger that would drive someone to the extremes of abandoning city life and the comforts of family and home in order to find a spiritual master whose guidance and holiness would provide a sure path to life in Christ. That profile includes docility, a willingness to submit to a rigid and demanding formation for the sake of growing in holiness.

Cassian explains Abba Isaac's way, and those who accepted Isaac as a spiritual father did exactly as he told them to do. While other brief formulas (what I am calling "little prayers") emerged through time, the principle remained the same. The "little prayer" reaches out toward God to ask for mercy, to offer oneself in readiness and service, and to keep oneself focused upon the presence of God in one's mind and heart.

By the end of the fifth century (especially in the East), the "little prayer" most commonly used by Christians seeking a contemplative life was the Jesus Prayer: "Lord Jesus Christ, Son of God; have mercy on me." Various fragments from the Psalms likewise became commonly used in this way, such as these phrases:

> Have mercy on me, God, in your goodness; in your great mercy blot out my sins. (Ps 51:1)

> Create a clean heart in me, O God; put a new and upright spirit within me. (Ps 51:10)

> In you, O Lord, I take refuge; never let me be put to shame. (Ps 71:1)

Other fragments from the Bible also proved to be inspiring and directive, such as these:

Lord, you know everything; you know that I love you. (John 21:17)

Behold the servant of the Lord; be it done unto me according to your word. (Luke 1:38)

Who will rescue me from this body of death? Thanks be to God through Jesus Christ our Lord! (Rom 7:24-5)

If God is for us, who can be against us? (Rom 8:31)

I believe; help my unbelief! (Mark 9:24)

Father, into your hands I commend my spirit. (Luke 23:46)

Maranatha: Come, Lord Jesus; Come! (Rev 22:20)

Today, many Christians have learned to offer their own "little prayers." The function of this tradition, especially in the busy lives of twenty-first century men and women, is to sustain a trusting and loving dialogue with God throughout our complex and overcharged days. Such little prayers might include, "Lord, be present to me in my work and my weariness"; "Loving God, take this busy day as a sign of my love for you"; "God, grant me strength to be patient (with these children . . . , with my pain today . . . , with the worry my spouse is causing me. . . .): I trust you to help me do what is loving and just." Simply, crisply, such prayers assist us in offering our life as it is.

For a serious Christian, these prayers of offering and intentionality provide the vehicle for a life of constant self-offering. They are the solution to the puzzle of how the Holy Spirit's anointing transmutes our humble and ordinary actions into spiritual sacrifices in solidarity with Christ's self-offering to his Father. Each of these "little prayers" is, in its own way, an act of *epiclesis,* invoking the Holy Spirit to transform our life, work, and prayer into an expression of the priestly mission of our baptismal priesthood. By this grace of the Holy Spirit, we are able to offer to God lives lifted in praise.

PRIESTLY ACTIONS FOR A PRIESTLY PEOPLE

It is fitting here to be reminded that the ordained have a crucial role to play in the formation of those living the baptismal priesthood. Everything that we have said in the preceding pages presupposes the support of the ordained ministry of our bishops and priests. As we noted in chapter 4, citing §1547 of the Catechism, ". . . the ministerial priesthood is at the service of the common priesthood. It is directed at the unfolding of the baptismal grace of all Christians. The ministerial priesthood is the *means* by which Christ unceasingly builds up and leads his church."

The faithful need their priests to be competent to assist them in their theological and spiritual formation. In the vision of Vatican II, the church is about mission and its apostolic frontiers are in the hands of the laity. For this vision to be fulfilled, the laity will need to be helped to understand more clearly their dignity as a priestly people and their role as agents of the Gospel's engagement with society. In the words of Pope John Paul II, "The more the lay apostolate develops, the more strongly is perceived the need to have well-formed holy priests. . . . The more the laity's own sense of vocation is deepened, the more what is proper to the priest stands out."[9] Through the sacrament of holy orders, the Holy Spirit "configures priests in a special way to Jesus Christ the Head and Shepherd; he forms and strengthens them with his pastoral charity; and gives them an authoritative role in the Church as servants of the proclamation of the Gospel to every people and of the fullness of Christian life of all the baptized."[10]

These statements of Pope John Paul from his 1992 apostolic letter on the ordained priesthood help us to see the strong missionary character of the ministerial priesthood. First and foremost, it is the role of the ordained to evangelize the Christian people in their care. This evangelization includes, of course, all the aspects of adult faith formation or mystagogy that we referred to in chapter 6. Each priest who is a pastor is configured to Christ as head of the local church that is Christ's body in the particular place where he is appointed. The pastor exercises his charism of "headship" by forming his people in an understanding of their baptismal priesthood. This is why Pope John Paul writes that "The ministry of the priest is entirely on behalf of the Church; it aims at promoting the exercise of the common priesthood of the entire people of God . . ."[11]

Concretely, the laity need effective leadership in the parish assembly, particularly in Sunday preaching, which is the broadest weekly contact between the pastor and the faithful. Missionary preaching in the parish begins with the Lectionary and moves into the family and the neighborhood. It reaches into the heart of Christ's gospel message to bring forth a grace and a challenge that the faithful will carry with them back to their homes and their workplace. The Sunday Eucharist needs to be celebrated in such a way that the "realized mystery" of Christ's Body in all the faithful is understood as the continuation throughout the week of what the people celebrate at the parish altar on Sunday.

To whatever degree possible, the activities of the parish's catechetical ministries, adult faith formation, social ministry, and community-building should be named, prayed for, and celebrated in the parish assembly. Finally, we should celebrate the dismissal of the community explicitly and vibrantly as a sending out on mission. A small Free Gospel Church in South Bend has signs on the exit ramps of its parking lots for departing Sunday congregants to notice as they drive away. The signs say: "You are entering mission territory!" Good advice for a priestly people!

LIVING THE REALIZED MYSTERY OF THE EUCHARIST THROUGHOUT THE DAY

In examining the "priestly" mission of the common priesthood, we have seen a kind of synthesis of everything that we have been working to articulate so far. Christ's priesthood in the presence of his Father has replaced all the bloody sacrifices of the ancient religions and of the Hebrew Temple with his own perfect sacrifice of himself, willingly offered in obedience to the One who sent him to be the source of our salvation. His self-offering on the cross and his lying in the tomb in death were a complete oblation of his life—a life at once divine and human. Before he went to his death, he left us the holy signs of our participation in his paschal mystery—baptism, first, and then especially the banquet of our salvation. This is celebrated with his Body and Blood under the graced sign of consecrated bread and wine; and by the invocation of the Spirit, those who eat of this sacrament become themselves "one body, one spirit in Christ"—the realized mystery of the Eucharist.

Through baptism and the gift of the Holy Spirit, we are offered the possibility of yielding over our lives and our individual destiny and taking on Christ's life and destiny as our own. In the language of the Bible and of the liturgy, we become members of his body. We live no longer for ourselves but for him.

This baptismal transformation makes possible our participation in his heavenly priesthood. What Christ offers to the Father in the liturgy of heaven is the treasure of his incarnation—his whole life and ministry—and together with that he offers also the faithful and loving actions of the members of his Body. We call these "spiritual sacrifices" in the language of 1 Peter 2, because that phrase refers to the faithful's sanctification by the anointing of the Holy Spirit and to their willing offering of their lives as members of Christ's Body.

This is the core meaning of the priesthood of the baptized. As members of Christ's body, we can simply offer life as it is, in all its complexity of successes and failures, sadness and joys, hopes and expectations. By entering consciously and intentionally into this mystery, we can both touch the world around us with the grace of Christ and offer to the Father, in the name of the Lord, the engagement of the Gospel with the needs of the world. Through lives that become unified through mindfulness and intentionality, through attention and holy desire, we enter into a great intimacy with Christ as we become vehicles of his sacramental presence in society. Our surrender to this mystery, our growth in generosity, and our willing sacrifice of ourselves to be faithful to the mystery of Christ gradually transform our lives. Our gift of ourselves, our holocaust offering, is nothing less than our whole lives lifted in praise and obedience throughout the course of what our duties, our relationships, and our initiatives for the wellbeing of the world unfold before us.

We are called to be a priestly people. Along with Christ, we can offer *our* whole "incarnation," that is, the becoming flesh of our faith and our love in our life of witness, to the Father. Here is the formula for a living church: a Body of Christ everywhere and always alive in the Holy Spirit for the sake of a world incandescent with love.

Notes

1. See Clive Thompson, "There's a Sucker Born in Every Medial Prefrontal Cortex," *The New York Times Magazine* (Oct. 26, 2003) 54–7.

2. The formula of The Apostolate of Prayer, which I learned as a child, was this: "O Jesus, through the Immaculate Heart of Mary, I offer you all my prayers, works, joys, and sufferings of this day in union with the Holy Sacrifice of the Mass throughout the world, in reparation for the sins of the world and in particular for . . . [and here the monthly intention of the Pope was inserted]." Notice the explicit link here between these ordinary actions as spiritual sacrifices and the celebration of the Eucharist. The absence of Trinitarian theology in this formula, however, is regrettable.

3. St. Thomas Aquinas, *Summa Theologiae*, Vol. 39 (2a2ae. 80–91), edited and trans. by Kevin D. O'Rourke, O.P. (New York: McGraw-Hill, 1964) 2a2ae, 83, 13, c–85.

4. Ibid., 83, 12, c–83.

5. *John Cassian: The Conferences*, Ancient Christian Writers, No. 57; trans. and annotated by Boniface Ramsey, O.P. (New York: Newman Press, 1997).

6. *John Cassian: The Institutes*, Ancient Christian Writers, No. 58; trans. and annotated by Boniface Ramsey, O.P. (New York: Newman Press, 2000).

7. *Cassian: Conferences*, op.cit., 375–6.

8. Ibid., 379.

9. Pope John Paul II, *Pastores Dabo Vobis (I Will Give You Shepherds)*, Apostolic Exhortation of March 25, 1992 (Washington, DC: United States Catholic Conference, 1992) 9 (n. 3).

10. Ibid., 39–40 (n. 15).

11. Ibid., 41 (n. 16).

Chapter *8*

An Intentional Symbolic Life

Years ago, in his last public audience, Pope Pius XI is reported to have described the Church as manifesting a deformed presence to the world: "The Church, the mystical Body of Christ, has become a monstrosity. The head is very large, but the body is shrunken."[1] Does this astonishing image apply equally well to the Church in our day?

The ministerial priesthood, especially the college of bishops, represents the "head" of the Body of Christ. Bishops and presbyters are the ordained leaders for the Church's evangelization, sanctification, and transforming mission; but their sacred powers lose their meaning unless they are "bodied forth" by an apostolic laity. The head has not done its job well if the rest of the body is not alert, vigorous, and engaged in the common mission of the Body of Christ. If ecclesial life is focused too prominently on the head, the Body of Christ becomes misshapen and, to use Pius's phrase, "shrunken." The Pope added, "the only way that you can rebuild it is to mobilize the lay people. You must call upon the lay people to become, along with you, the witnesses of Christ."[2]

Pius XI's imagery is prophetic and revealing, but it touches only one aspect of the mystery of Christians' new life in Christ, their missionary instinct. Equally important, perhaps more important, is their consciousness of their intimate union with Christ, their growth in a spiritual life. They are, after all, the social sacrament of Christ' resurrection life; they are the church, that vital sign of the union of God with humanity.

People hunger to know that their lives have enduring meaning. The revelation that baptism offers us a completely new existence is good news indeed. But it can seem like nothing more than an adult

132

fairy tale for Sunday mornings unless it blossoms into the daily, intentional grasp of the Christian mystery which is the living priesthood of the baptized. How can Christians come to comprehend this vocation more clearly? I submit that the answer lies in integrating faith with daily life. The way we think about things affects the way we live, so I would like to talk a bit here about imagination.

I have found the terms *symbolic* and *diabolic* useful to designate opposing dynamics in the imagination. Although I use these words in a sense that differs from popular usage, my meaning is faithful to the root sense of the words. Both *symbolic* and *diabolic* are compound terms formed from the same Greek root *(bolein)* meaning to throw or cast. However one begins with the prefix *sym*, which means together, while the other begins with *dia*, which means apart. A symbol throws things together. A diabolic force casts them apart.[3] These terms may be useful in interpreting the practical meaning of baptismal priesthood. In chapter 5, we made note of Cardinal Newman's distinction between the *notional* and the *real*. It seems to me that we can pair the diabolic with the notional, on the one hand, and the symbolic with the real, on the other hand.

What binds or holds together the random experience of day-to-day reality with the experience of faith is symbolic imagination. As ordinary people involved with familiar things, we are asked to accord space and welcome to the divine. God can enter any moment or any activity of ours and become integrated with our sense of the real. Symbolic imagination can connect any moment's fragmentary reality with the deep mystery of our new life in God. This is exactly what baptismal priesthood asks of us; namely, to link the events and consciousness of every day to our union with Christ as members of his living body on earth.

By contrast, diabolic imagination, manifested in the attitude that Christianity is what we do in church on Sunday, severs the ordinary from the transcendent. When this happens, religious meaning becomes compartmentalized into a sacred parenthesis which interrupts the flow of daily experience. The diabolic imagination aspires to domesticate transcendence by setting it apart and, in doing so, to control and tame it. Diabolic images are a mere caricature of authentic mystery—mere "notions" to use the language of Cardinal Newman. We can be vehemently insistent about our ideas of orthodoxy and spirituality and still relate to them as nothing more than ideas. In this way, the Spirit's transforming action is short-circuited and so cut off from the flow of our ordinary experiences.

I have titled this book *The Priesthood of the Faithful: Key to a Living Church* in order to stress the unity between genuine human living and the mystery of our life in Christ. The priesthood of the faithful is not bracketed into ritual actions or periodic moments of heightened consciousness. It is integral to a life lived symbolically—vitally joined in faith and love to the resurrection reality of our Lord who never ceases to invite us to deeper and deeper discipleship.

As a new era of Christian life dawns, the doctrine of Christ's priesthood can serve as a compass to show us where we are headed. As we have observed, the church's ministry, in North America at least, is being impacted by a number of factors, including a shortage of priests and a growing guild of skilled and effective Lay Ecclesial Ministers. In the midst of these transformations, we seem to have some confusion about what our pastoral goals really are. Is the aim of Catholic pastoral practice the apostolic laity envisaged by so many of the documents of Vatican II or, by contrast, must we be contented with maintaining past generations' practice of ministry marked in many ways by clericalism and condescension toward the laity?

In the midst of all the pressures upon the church today, a new force is gradually emerging. This force is linked to the growing hunger of Catholics for a more meaningful Christian life. It manifests itself in the craving of serious Catholics for good preaching, and in the generosity of many laypersons engaged in apostolic works, both recognized and unrecognized, both professional and volunteer. This new force is also expressed in the growing interest of lay Catholics in the church's traditional customs, theology, and spiritual practices. They would be a ready audience for adult faith formation, if only more ministers of the church were fully prepared to provide it.

We are observing, as it were, a change of seasons. Think of the eagerness with which we observe the signs of springtime at the end of a long winter. Even while the nights remain cold, the brightening sun coaxes trees and bushes to put forth their buds. We watch these tiny signs of life fatten, then gradually open into the warming light of the early spring sun. Even before the blossoms open, we anticipate the beauty of what they promise.

Christ is the vine and we are the branches. The rising sap in the branches is the gift of the Holy Spirit infusing believers with a deep desire for a richer Christian life. As the Spirit gave energizing direction to the bishops at the Second Vatican Council, so today the Spirit's gift of understanding is illuminating the church's insight into its participation in the priesthood of Christ. I believe that a new age of spirituality and evangelization is about to blossom.

The previous chapters have attempted to describe this new life force in the Catholic world in careful steps. We examined initiation into Christ's priesthood through baptism and then explored the sacramental existence of the Christian faithful in chapters 1 to 4. Then we examined the "prophetic," "royal," and "priestly" dimensions of baptismal priesthood in chapters 5 to 7. All these topics could be explored in considerably more detail. However, our chief goal in this book has been to make the case as clearly and simply as possible that every baptized Christian has a vocation to a life that is both apostolic and contemplative. What is more, these dimensions of the Christian life are rooted in the faithful's participation in Christ's eternal priesthood.

In this concluding chapter, I shall attempt to summarize the ways in which a correct theological understanding of the common priesthood provides a greater depth of meaning and direction for lay Catholics, then for Lay Ecclesial Ministers, and finally for bishops and priests. We shall see that at the heart of the church's life the people of God are already strategically inserted in the world as a dynamic force with the potential to transform it into the kingdom of God. By living their lives "symbolically," that is, by bringing their faith and their spiritual gifts into everything they are and do, Christians can become a powerful "benign contagion" in society. In our day the challenge for the faithful is to recognize and own the gifts of the Spirit that have been won for them.

A FLOURISHING, FAITHFUL PEOPLE

A flourishing laity are first of all people who know that they are loved and who feel important in the life of the church. We find in 1 Peter an appeal to the newly initiated to appreciate their value in the life of the church. "You are a chosen race, a royal priesthood, a holy nation, God's own people, in order that you may proclaim the mighty acts of him who called you out of darkness into his marvelous light" (2:9).

At the very beginning of Christianity, the disciples of the risen, newly absent Christ were persuaded that their own lives were a treasure in the eyes of God, and that they personally and individually were known and loved. They knew that they were chosen by God. Their presence and influence in the world were meant to be a source of light for others. They were called to continue the ministry of prophecy and healing that their Savior Jesus Christ began. They knew that they were essential to the mission of the church.

This Christian message has not changed. Peter's statement applies just as much to us as to the people who first heard it. Using the theology of the common priesthood of the baptized as our lens, today's Christians can see how the teaching of 1 Peter is an open invitation to express God's redeeming mercies in the ways we think and live, choose and act. The power of Christ's transforming grace and the intimacy of our relation with him will be expressed in the radiance of our convictions and our generosity. As Jesus gave his life for us so that we can have his eternal life, we offer our lives and energies to him so that he can express in us the transforming work of the new creation.

First Peter uses a gripping expression: "You know that you were ransomed from the futile ways inherited from your ancestors, not with perishable things like silver or gold, but with the precious blood of Christ . . ." (1:18-19) Peter's reference to "futile ways" referred to the futility of pagan sacrifices and even those of the Jewish temple. Blood sacrifices cannot save us. They cannot sanctify our lives. Christians are ransomed from the futility of bloody sacrifices, as we saw in the last chapter, by the new covenant in which Christ presents to his Father the living offerings, the spiritual sacrifices, of his disciples.

For us today, "futile ways" has other meanings. Let us consider work, for example. In a culture in which people work harder and longer than their parents with less hope of achieving the affluence of their parents' generation, futility can be readily linked to feelings of pointlessness. Fewer workers today maintain the same occupation throughout a lifetime; fewer still remain with the same employer or company for decades. The family feeling that enhanced the communal meaning of work in a lifelong relationship to a company or a team of workers, not to mention a family farm, is very rare today. Consequently work easily appears as a purely instrumental means of earning a living, without much human or spiritual significance.

What political philosophers in the last century referred to as "alienation" is still a reality for many people today. Karl Marx coined the term "alienation" as a description of the sense of disconnection between workers and work as the expression of their personality.[4] This happens in industrial, assembly-line work where each person contributes only a small and often disconnected fragment in the whole production process. The worker leaves no "fingerprints" upon the finished product, to use a suggestive image. The person is "alienated" from the product that he or she has made.

A similar sense of disconnection may afflict professionals such as insurance brokers, money managers, lawyers or doctors who deal with huge numbers of cases. The relational link that gives human meaning to work becomes either broken or so attenuated that its significance is lost. People become numbers, and numbers do not tell stories or become friends. When work loses its human dimension, it becomes impersonal and mechanical.

By giving work a spiritual meaning, Christians can restore its life-giving dimensions without necessarily altering the conditions of work. Maintaining a perspective of care and a purpose of enabling life can make a huge difference in the feeling one has for one's job. We all know persons who have discovered how to transform impersonal tasks into friendly and cheering human encounters. Such people not only give human meaning to those whom they serve; they also receive meaning and joy themselves from a humanizing exercise of their responsibilities. Making one's work a conscious part of one's spiritual life ransoms it from futility.

Two aspects of the Christian theology of baptismal priesthood are particularly relevant here. First of all, the workers' self-investment and toil can be integrated into their obedience to the vocation that they have received. This stems from Christians' sense of purpose in offering the gifts they have received from God in a way that is generous and gracious. When helping to settle an insurance claim, one may extend a sympathetic feeling for the other person's plight. When performing factory labor, one may cultivate a spirit of comradeship with fellow workers, perhaps infusing the often boring and monotonous process of repetitive actions with a sense of humor or even simply maintaining a spirit of mutual respect in a situation of personal friction. Gestures of care, respect, and integrity can flow from Christian workers' recognition that their actions are always somehow interpersonal in the sense of affecting positively or negatively the lives of others. An enlivening presence to others in this way becomes a vehicle for the breaking in of the Kingdom of God.

Second, as we have seen above, the theology of the common priesthood allows us to understand how our lives, expressed in our work and attitudes, become united to the Christian community's offering of its life and meaning to God in the Eucharist. The integrity, patience, generosity, imagination, and love of Christian workers are the living expression of the Spirit of Christ. Christians should realize that at any given moment they are called, right where they are, to be salt and light, as Matthew 5 puts it, through the Holy Spirit's gifts of faith and love. Their spiritual sacrifices, as we have repeatedly called these expressions of their faith, are not only offerings which they offer "along with the body of the Lord," but are also a symbolic force that reveals the Spirit's action in the world.

The more our hunger for meaning is satisfied, the richer our spiritual life becomes. As Christians, our understanding of Christ's presence in the Eucharist will be proportional to our grasp of the reality of Christ's presence in our daily lives. If we think that the "real presence" of Christ in the consecrated bread and wine, the "graced sign" of the Eucharist, is the totality of the divine mystery that the church celebrates and "re-members," we are missing a lot. The "realized mystery" of the Eucharist, as I have repeatedly explained, is the goal or end of this sacrament and its effect in the world. Without an understanding of this realized mystery, which is Christ's presence in their *lives,* the faithful can fully understand neither what they celebrate, nor the gift they offer in the mystery of the Eucharist.

Conversely, for people whose lives have become eucharistic in the sense of the "realized mystery," the "graced sign" takes on a powerful depth of meaning and beauty. Put most simply, for them the Eucharist is not just a gift of God as nourishment and love (though it is surely that), but it is also the surrender and gift of themselves to the living mystery (the priesthood) of Christ. This gift of self is made concrete in the visible sign of saying "Amen" to the "Body of Christ" and of eating the Body and drinking the Blood of the Lord. The Eucharist becomes for them not only the sacrament of God's love toward them, but also a sacrament of their reciprocal response of love toward God.

POPULAR DEVOTIONS AND LAY PIETY

Good pastors are always on the lookout to find ways to link liturgy and life. Meanwhile, many Catholics are accustomed to rooting their faith experience in popular devotions such as family altars with holy pictures and statues. In their November 2003, pastoral statement on popular devotional practices, the U.S. bishops described popular devotions as an encounter between Catholic faith and the culture.[5] The bishops said that the liturgies of a healthy parish should overflow the structure of the Mass and the other sacraments to bring Christian worship into the homes and daily life of parishioners. Popular devotions ought to help the biblical faith and liturgical practice of the parish to spread its roots into the hearts of the people.

Especially in some immigrant communities, the role of popular devotions can be powerfully important. When members of Catholic families who have migrated here from abroad possess only a limited understanding of English, popular devotions in their own tongue can be a tremendous comfort. Even aside from the matter of language, however, the visual imagery and traditional melodies that people bring with them from their native cultures provide links that are reassuring and spiritually nurturing. It is easy enough to give examples. The image of Our Lady of Guadalupe evokes strong feelings, not only for Mexicans, but for most Latin American people. In the same way, statues or prints of Our Lady of Charity are fondly revered by Cuban Catholics. Popular images of this kind are often displayed prominently on family altars not only in Latin American homes, but also among Vietnamese, Filipino, and other immigrant Catholics.

Sometimes popular devotions have a communal and folkloric quality to them, as in the case of *Las Posadas*. This is an Hispanic devotion in which members of the parish pass through their neighborhoods and knock at the doors of parishioners, representing the journey of Mary and Joseph seeking a shelter for the birth of their divine child. Likewise, customs that celebrate Asian New Year also involve prayers and festivities that blend faith and fellowship. In line with the bishops' recommendations, we should be looking for opportunities to promote this kind of solidarity in faith in our parishes whenever possible. Catholics whose families have been in the U.S. long enough to forget their ethnic traditions can surely benefit from the traditions and customs of more recently arrived Catholic immigrants, especially in the area of popular religiosity.

Other popular devotional practices with ethnic roots, such as the European advent wreath with its prayers and lighting of candles to symbolize the approach of Christmas, can also enrich the family's devotional life. The blessing of homes at Easter—once done in the small communities of Europe by the bishop or the priest—now begs for an adaptation in our present circumstances to a blessing presided over by a parish deacon, a lay ecclesial minister, or, perhaps, the parent-head of the household. The priestly mission of parents or community leaders who offer guidance to other Christians in common prayer includes drawing upon the creativity and shared traditions of the people who gather around them. The African American community, for instance, has a rich tradition of spontaneous prayer for the needs of the sick and the troubled.

New practices flowing from the experiences of small Christian communities or from the exercises of parish renewal programs should be promoted as well. In all these cases, the parish can find means to help families own and develop their identity as "domestic church," that is, as the fundamental unit in which the spirituality of baptismal priesthood takes hold.

As the bishops' pastoral statement makes clear, "Personal and family prayer and devotions should flow from and lead to a fuller participation in the liturgy. . . . [P]opular devotions should naturally be strongly imbued with biblical themes, language and imagery. . . ."[6] Pastors and communities who pay attention to the possibilities for promoting meaningful popular devotions in multicultural parishes will help immigrant parishioners begin to feel at home. Understanding and celebrating the popular piety of a particular people is a rich and gracious way to incorporate them into the community's life and worship. It is also a means of enriching the devotional life of fellow parishioners of different cultural backgrounds.

Household devotions are particularly beneficial to the Christian formation of children. Rituals that gather the family together with the lighting of candles, the recitation of prayers and singing of hymns, with readings from the stories of the Bible and words of blessing in the name of God, are strong, memorable experiences for the very young. Such acts of devotion can landscape the religious imagination of the child, planting imagery, feeling, and faith that will endure (even if it will change in some details) over a lifetime.[7] Through family prayer and devotions of this kind, the natural affections of children for their parents and close family members become linked to their religious affections and their sense of God in their lives.

Intergenerational concerns are as much a part of the church's pastoral responsibility as are multicultural concerns. Particularly important is the concern of grounding our children in a Catholic sensibility. Catholic popular devotions are one way to attend to this. Obviously the exact nature of these family devotions will vary considerably depending upon culture, class, and educational backgrounds. Catholic parents bear the primary responsibility for introducing family devotions into the life of the "domestic church." Pastors and parish religious education directors can assist parents in this task by providing them with examples of formulas for family prayer and catechesis.

EUCHARIST AS SHAPER
OF THE PRIESTLY PIETY OF THE FAITHFUL

The topic of popular devotions illustrates a reality that we have tended to overlook in recent years, namely, the desire of the laity to be connected to religious practices that register with their culture and experience. For many people, the rite of the Mass seems wordy, monotonous, and, to use a metaphor, antiseptic. Some complaints include the use of unfamiliar and difficult melodies for congregational singing, the proclamation of the Scriptures by readers who can scarcely pronounce the words of the text, and so-called preaching that settles for good-natured homespun advice or personal anecdotes about the priest's feelings in place of the vivid proclamation of revealed truth. These are all missed opportunities for connecting with the religious passions of the faithful. By turning the liturgy into a theatrical event of very dubious quality, they eviscerate it of its prophetic power.

The theology of the baptismal priesthood runs headlong into conflict with such mediocre pastoral practices. Presiders are wrong to think that the rite belongs to them personally and, to the degree that their attitude dispossesses the faithful of their active role, they are sinfully wrong. The lector who imagines that a tortured and unintelligible proclamation of an Old Testament lesson does not matter because the reading is a mere formal ornament in the celebration of Mass is also badly mistaken. Musicians who settle for performing music *at* Mass rather than eliciting the full-throated participation of the faithful in the sung rites *of* the Mass conspire to rob the faithful of their heritage. Such malpractice is so commonplace these days that calling attention to it most often elicits annoyance rather than correction.

Unless these dynamics of Christian celebration are rectified, the most powerful means that the Church has for the theological formation of the faithful as a priestly people are being used at cross-purposes—deforming rather than forming an apostolic Body of Christ. This is a tragedy. It goes against God's desire for the church. The laity are meant to be sacraments of Christ's grace in the world. Their faith and witness are an irreplaceable dynamic influence. In order for them to exercise their beneficial influence in the world, the laity must come to recognize and own their priestly identity. In every way, the church's pastoral practice must be aimed at helping them to achieve this witness.

Here is the place to note the priestly leadership of parents and lay leaders who undertake to lead their families or small communities in prayer. This is an expression of the "priestly" charism of the common priesthood. It draws upon the sensitivity of the leader to support the faith and call forth the generosity of others. In households in which customs of regular family prayer are common, this priestly action is a powerful blessing for the family members. In small communities in which lay leaders offer prophetic and royal direction, their exercise of their baptismal priesthood becomes a true grace for others.

Every Christian is recruited by faith and discipleship to exercise a dynamic, visible role as a symbolic-sacramental representative of the heavenly Christ. This priesthood is prophetic in appreciating and expressing (however simply) the conviction that Christ lives on in the church through us. It is royal in mobilizing the vigor and enthusiasm of life in commitment to the Gospel and its values. It is priestly in its grateful offering of life's very purpose to the activity of the Spirit of Christ in works of justice, love, and peacemaking.

Sharing Christ's priesthood is God's plan for us. It is an immense dignity. In carrying out this plan, we will find both meaning and happiness. It is both the greatest blessing we will ever receive and the greatest blessing that we will ever be able to offer to others.

THE FAITHFUL AS FULL-TIME APOSTLES

We turn now to Lay Ecclesial Ministers (LEMs). How can the theology of the common priesthood increase our understanding of the important role of LEMs in the life of the church and offer to them a more penetrating appreciation of their distinctive vocation? To try to answer this question, I would like to begin with some important background.

In the first half of the twentieth century, since the church's mission or ministry was seen as pertaining to the hierarchy, the term "Lay Apostolate" was used to refer to the public actions of the faithful on behalf of the church. The term "Catholic Action" was also used to describe the participation of the laity in the apostolate of the hierarchy. The apostolate of the ordained was conceived essentially with reference to the internal ministry of sanctification and governance of the church itself. In the late 1920s, Pope Pius XI began to develop a missionary perspective for the laity, challenging them to be the bearers of Christian values and social principles to the world of work and politics.[8]

In mid-century, the Second Vatican Council went further in re-shaping the agenda for ecclesial life. In the Council's vision, the church's fundamental mission is not to itself, but to the world and to the nations;[9] the church is missionary in its fundamental purpose.[10] The faithful's entitlement to mission is not by delegation from the hierarchy, but is conveyed by the Spirit through the sacraments of baptism, confirmation, and Eucharist. The threefold mission of Christ to teach, sanctify, and guide is not extended to bishops and priests alone by the sacrament of orders, but to all the faithful by the sacraments of baptism and confirmation.

These substantial theological developments in the Council's ecclesiology led to a diversity of opinions by the time the document on the laity was drafted in the last session of the Council. Some bishops thought that there was no need for a separate document on the laity, while others wanted an exhaustive study of the ways in which the laity could be apostolically involved.[11] Eventually the Council issued the Decree on the Apostolate of Lay People, which summarized rather succinctly the majority theological vision that emerged from the Council's deliberations:

- Lay apostolic work flows from the faithful person's vocation as a Christian; the Council wants to foster lay apostolic activity by the faithful. (AA n. 1)
- Every activity of the mystical body that intends to share in the saving work of redemption should go by the name of apostolate; "the Christian vocation is, of its nature, a vocation to the apostolate as well." (AA n. 2)
- Lay people too [meaning in addition to the ordained], sharing in the priestly, prophetical and kingly office of Christ, play their part in the mission of the whole people of God in the church and in the world. (AA n. 2)
- The apostolate through which the faithful build the church, sanctify the world and call it to life in Christ, takes many different forms. (AA n. 16)

The document affirms that the "right and duty" of the faithful to be apostles arises from their identification with Christ in his mystical body through baptism and anointing in the Spirit (AA n. 3). The Holy Spirit sanctifies all the faithful and gives each of them gifts or charisms to be put at the service of others for the building up of the whole Body of Christ. All the faithful, with or without ordination or public religious vows, are made agents of prophecy and sanctification through their sacramental life. Christian believers who receive charisms from the Spirit are obliged to use them in the church and in the world.

This teaching pictures a vibrant and creative engagement between the baptized and all the relational and political structures of society. Not surprisingly, apostolic life began to flourish among the laity in the decades following the Council. However, the Council's teaching about a fruitful Christian life of faith and service has been followed by the Vatican's later expression of concern about the negative effect on the ordained of all this lay ecclesial action. I refer to the position, strongly affirmed by the Vatican in 1997, that the *ordained* participate in the mission of the church in *ministry, others* participate in the ministry of the ordained through *"apostolates"* or apostolic actions.[12] The term now officially proposed by the U.S. bishops for the faithful who are recognized as partners in ecclesial mission, "Lay Ecclesial Ministers," is neuralgic for some Roman Curial officials. The 1997 Vatican Instruction states that "it should be clearly noted that only in virtue of sacred ordination does the work [ministry] obtain that full, univocal meaning that tradition has attributed to it."[13] What is going on here? It will be useful to quickly identify some of the dimensions of this question.

Given the new parameters of Vatican II, the problem for a number of officials in the Roman Curia became, "On what basis are the distinctiveness and superiority of ordained ministry in the Church maintained?" At the release of the 1997 instruction, Vatican officials noted that "lay ministries that obscure the differences between ordained priests and the laity, even if motivated by a desire to serve priestless communities, are harmful to the church."[14] Archbishop (now Cardinal) Dario Castrillon Hoyos, the key sponsor of the 1997 Instruction, remarked that the document "provides norms to overcome the phenomenon of the clericalization of the laity and the secularization of the clergy."[15] Notably absent from the document or from any of the remarks of Vatican officials about it was reference to the urgent need of Catholic parish communities worldwide for pastoral leadership in light of the diminished supply of ordained ministers.

There is also the lingering question about the meaning of the essential difference (not only a difference in degree) between the common priesthood of the faithful and the ministerial priesthood. This important phrase of the Constitution on the Church, n. 10, that we have observed in various places throughout this book has never been definitively interpreted. Number 10 suggests a meaning for the "essential" difference in ordained priesthood by saying that "the ministerial priest, by the sacred power that he has, forms and governs the priestly people; in the person of Christ he brings about the Eucharistic sacrifice and offers it to God in the name of all the people." As to the faithful, in virtue of their "royal priesthood," they too share in the offering of the Eucharist and "they exercise that priesthood by the reception of the sacraments, by prayer and thanksgiving, by the witness of a holy life, self denial and active charity."

This proposed solution is less than satisfying in that by its structure it suggests a dichotomy. That, of course, cannot possibly be the case. Otherwise ministerial priests would not exercise their own common priesthood by the reception of the sacraments, prayer and thanksgiving, a holy life, self-denial, and charity. The failure of this and other magisterial texts in recent years to arrive at a clear distinction between the ordained and the church's other faithful people without removing bishops and priests from the dynamics of the common priesthood is ultimately very confusing.

The Vatican's distinction discussed here attempts to create a juridical solution, answering a penetrating question with a simple authoritarian decree. However, we have already seen that a sacramental solution works well enough within the logic of the theology of the Council. Christians are living sacraments of Christ. We can think of the ordained as representing Christ in the manner of a "graced sign" as the *means* of salvation, whereas the faithful's common priesthood (which obviously includes the ordained as well) represents Christ in the manner of a "realized mystery," as the *fruit* of our salvation.

We have mentioned this approach before, one that was proposed by French theologian Daniel Bourgeois, as we noted in chapter 4. In the next section, we will see that it appears to be clearly in harmony with recent papal teaching. But even with it there are some problems. Why would we deny to Lay Ecclesial Ministers (LEMs) the qualification of acting as "graced signs," that is, as *means* of sanctification, when they act in the name of Christ in their prophetic teaching or their pastoral guidance of individuals and groups? Like the ordained, they are faithful disciples, in one respect, and apostolic workers, in another respect (even if some in the Roman Curia would deny them the title "ministers"). Their apostolic action is truly a work of discipleship and Christian love arising from the movement of the Holy Spirit. They are clearly in this respect "graced signs" in the sense given to the ordained priest whose ministry they share.

How does baptismal priesthood illuminate lay ecclesial ministry? How does this teaching help the church to see what it is becoming?

LAY ECCLESIAL MINISTRY AS THE FULL FLOWERING OF BAPTISMAL PRIESTHOOD

Let us move beyond considering theory to examining practice. Catholic theologian Susan Wood, in presenting the proceedings of the Collegeville Ministry Seminar, reported the points of convergence that express the consensus of the seminar's participants. Her first point is that "Theologies of ministry must begin with an experiential description of ministry today."[16] Thirty thousand Lay Ecclesial Ministers are providing the church in the U.S. with the skills, love, and service that make Catholic ministry possible in our expanding church population. Today there are more than 3,150 parishes without resident pastors in the U.S. Some bishops have begun mandating that new church buildings must accommodate massive numbers. Some suburban parishes already register as many as ten thousand families. To conduct theological reflection on Catholic ministry without taking into account these important facts is simply not responsible. Clearly the Catholic Church in North America will be able to fulfill its mission in its present circumstances only through the generous and effective pastoral service of LEMs.

Wood continues with an excellent summary of how baptism is the source of all ministry: "Baptism initiates a person as member of the community, and ministry arises from the community." As we have seen, all the baptized share in Christ's priesthood in diverse ways. All ministry, ordained and lay, proceeds from baptism. "[T]he most fundamental ordering of the Church occurs in baptism. [Through it] we assume our place in the order of the Church according to a state in life and the charisms we bring for the upbuilding of the community and Christian discipleship."[17]

The theology of the common priesthood allows us to link our radical transformation through baptism with the sanctifying, prophetic, and pastoral missions of Christ exercised in the church by his members. As Wood puts it, "We must find a way to locate all ministry as the ministry of the Church before it is the ministry of an individual, whether that person be ordained or non-ordained. . . . We must find a way to recognize this work of the laity in the Church as ecclesial, that is, the ministry of the entire Church and not just that of an individual baptized Christian."[18]

The point here is that, whether we use the word *ministry* or *apostolate*, there is work being done by the faithful that is not just a hobby or part-time job, but is a true charism and must be recognized as such. The pastoral action of LEMs arises out of their own sacramental life, that is, out of their relationship with Christ in the Holy Spirit. The faith and charisms that they express in ecclesial ministry are the action of the Holy Spirit within their own persons. This means that their exercise of ministry will be marked by their own personalities, including their sensibilities and creativity. In this sense, their ministry is deeply personal. However, this does not differ from the experience of the ordained. For LEMs and priests, their human circumstances, family background, achievements, interests, and personal qualities are not obstacles to their pastoral action, but instruments for their effective ministry.

What distinguishes the experience of LEMs is that their pastoral action is not exercised independently, but in concert with the charisms of the ordained. Here is a case where the concept of right relationship comes into play. Church order is a sacrament of unity and that demands a principle of leadership. The headship of the community belongs to ordained, recognized leaders. Ordination and this recognition no longer always go hand in hand; priests are not organically called forth from their own communities as in the earliest days of the church.

LEMs are assistants to priests, as priests are canonical assistants to the bishop. For LEMs, as for priests and bishops, the internal principles of faith and charism are the source of their teaching, guidance, and leadership in prayer in the ecclesial ministry of the parish and the diocese. Their pastoral ministry and service are authentic realizations of Christ's sacramental presence in the life of the church.

When necessary, LEMs, rather than merely assisting pastors, may be appointed to stand in for them. This intensification of Christian discipleship is also a call to deeper intimacy with Christ. In the chapter on baptism, we noted the vocation of the faithful to divinization, the transformation into a deeper and deeper likeness to Christ. Every Christian is called to become penetrated by the Word of God and the Spirit of Christ. That general vocation becomes all the more insistent and urgent in the case of those chosen for ecclesial leadership, such as LEMs, just as it obviously does for priests and bishops.

Given the still emerging nature and structure of this leadership in the era of the post-Vatican II church, LEMs can be assured that they will face many sources of moral and spiritual purification. They will need to be patient with the ambiguity of their role, caught as they are between the people they serve and the ordained leaders to whom they report in pastoral administration. They will occasionally know suffering caused by needlessly complex protocols of administration as the church works out its self-understanding in a new age of ministry. And in many cases, LEMs will know insecurity in their tenure and inadequacy in their finances. Nonetheless, what is marvelous in my experience is to discover again and again how many LEMs know this, and still regard their vocation as worth all the effort.

LEMs are themselves ministers of unity. Their competence, passion, and love of God's people will lead them to recognize their extraordinary role in the life of a church very much in a state of evolution. Like the helpers of Paul listed lovingly at the end of his pastoral letters to the churches of the ancient world, today's LEMs are the tenders of the fire of the Holy Spirit in the lives of local communities. Their cooperation in the ministry of the church will evolve into a new structure of ecclesial vitality and promote a renaissance of spiritual life in the churches. As both lay faithful and ecclesial leaders, LEMs model baptismal priesthood in its full flowering. They are providing the foundation of support that makes the ministerial priesthood viable and fruitful in the special circumstances of a growing Catholic population and a diminishing ministerial priesthood.

A DELICATE DANCE IN THE POWER OF THE SPIRIT

In October of 2003, Pope John Paul released a lengthy document called an "apostolic exhortation" that summarizes the work of the Synod of Bishops held in 2001 at the Vatican. Entitled "*Pastores Gregis:* Shepherds of the Flock," the apostolic exhortation discusses the qualities of a bishop, his teaching role, and his dialogue and collaboration with others in the local church and beyond. Paragraph n. 10 of this document is of particular interest here, because it discusses the theme of the priesthood of the baptized. This passage is so rich that I shall quote it in full:

> The interplay between the common priesthood of the faithful and the ministerial priesthood, present in the episcopal ministry itself, is manifested in a kind of *perichoresis* [interplay] between the two forms of priesthood: a *perichoresis* between the common witness to the faith given by the faithful and the bishop's authoritative witness

to the faith through his magisterial acts; a *perichoresis* between the lived holiness of the faithful and the means of sanctification that the bishop offers them; and finally, a *perichoresis* between the personal responsibility of the bishop for the good of the church entrusted to him and the shared responsibility of all the faithful for that same church.[19]

This unusual word, *perichoresis*, is compounded of the Greek, *peri-* (around), and *khoros* (dance). Its use as a technical term in theology developed in the eighth century as theologians struggled to understand how God could be both one and three—one divine reality expressed in three distinct persons who are not, however, three separate realities (or natures) but only one God. In its technical, theological use, *perichoresis* means mutually inhering in one another and drawing life from one another. It affirms that while the Son proceeds from the Father, the Son is also contained in the Father; and while the Spirit proceeds from the Father and Son, the Spirit is equal to them both and is contained in them. It is not surprising, then, that the metaphor of dance is used to describe this interaction of the divine persons. This image suggests that the divine persons' relationships and creative economy of grace is more like play than work. One theologian describes the term *perichoresis* as expressing "the pure creativity of uncreated freedom and love."[20]

Given this background, it is quite interesting that Pope John Paul II used this word in the apostolic exhortation to express the relationship of baptismal and ministerial priesthood. It points to the equal dignity of these two expressions of Christ's priesthood and their mutual dependence one upon the other: "The fact that for all their difference in essence each is ordered to the other gives rise to an interplay that harmoniously structures the life of the Church as the place where the salvation brought about by Christ is made historically present."[21]

This teaching offers real insight for the exercise of the ministerial priesthood, particularly to bishops. Three main points emerge from the paragraph quoted above. First mentioned is the interplay between the common witness of the faithful (with all that this suggests about the evangelization of culture) and the bishop's authoritative witness. This point highlights the effective primacy of the prophetic mission of bishops in the administration of their churches. As we have repeatedly seen, the ecclesiology of this new age focuses upon the apostolic laity's transforming influence in the world. It is incumbent upon bishops to provide leadership in catechesis, especially adult faith formation, that will enable the apostolic laity to perform effectively. In addition to catechesis, substantive and engaging preaching looms large as a necessity for a fully functioning local church. The bishops must see that their priests are equipped for this task. The apostolic exhortation puts these priorities into focus in an unmistakable way.

Second, the document speaks of the interplay between the lived holiness of the faithful and the means of sanctification that the bishop offers them. As we noted above in chapter 6, drawing upon the U.S. bishops' own document on adult faith formation, the most effective means for forming the faithful in holiness is the formation of small Christian communities or cells for common study and prayer. Exhortations, explanations, documents, and legislation have a very limited impact on the experience of the faithful without the help of some relational social structures to mediate their engagement through conversation, study, and dialogue.

This insight may help bishops and priests to focus their energies on holiness-promoting efforts that respect the conceptual and social dynamics of those being sanctified. Lest priests and bishops panic at the thought of creating and administering myriad small groups, it may be calming to know that thousands of such groups already exist and are self-sustaining. They have arisen from diverse origins such as Cursillo, Marriage Encounter, the Charismatic Renewal, Teams of Our Lady, and the Renew Program, to name a few. With only a small amount of encouragement (and perhaps a few tips on what helps a group survive), adult laypeople are entirely capable of forming and running without supervision the small groups that can provide them with sustaining, faith-filled companionship through the years.

In the third place, the apostolic exhortation speaks of the interplay of the personal responsibility of the bishop for the good of the church and the shared responsibility of all the faithful. This statement is a real ecclesiological development, in my view. Naturally bishops who are good pastors have always called upon the faithful to assist them in various ways in ministering to the needs of the diocese. However, this image of *perichoresis*—a mutually enriching interplay of energies—represents something new, I think. For bishops and pastors, it poses questions concerning how the faithful can assist them in strengthening and guiding Christian institutions (universities, schools, hospitals, agencies for social service, etc.), drawing upon the charisms and expertise of laity who are professionally competent in appropriate areas.

This is not the place to attempt a programmatic exploration of the potential of this idea, given the scope of this topic. However, a genuine co-responsibility of bishop and faithful—of ministerial priesthood and common priesthood—obviously points in the direction of a sustained dialogue about pastoral priorities, mutual respect for the differing competencies of the two sides of the equation, and an earnest agenda-setting to make structures of co-responsibility also structures for the recruitment of the talents and energies of the faithful in a diocese or a parish.

The theology developed in this book finds many indications of confirmation and support in *Pastores Gregis*. This papal document is in clear harmony with the interpretation of the ministerial priesthood as a "graced sign" or *means* of sanctification and of the baptismal priesthood as the "realized mystery" or *goal* of Christ's ministry, as we have often phrased the matter. Likewise this document recognizes the essential and critical role of catechetical and pastoral formation for the faithful, precisely because the lay faithful are in most instances the point of engagement between the church and the culture.

It is impossible to read *Pastores Gregis* and maintain an interpretation of ministerial priesthood as exclusively cultic, that is, as overwhelmingly concerned with liturgical ceremonies. The ministerial priesthood is comprehensive—prophetic, pastoral, and also liturgical. Priests and people both have their critical roles to play in bringing the church alive in the world. To cite the document once again, "These are obviously two relationships which do not simply stand side-by-side but are deeply interconnected; . . . two modes of participation in the one priesthood of Christ, which involves two dimensions which unite in the supreme act of the sacrifice of the cross."[22]

The sacred dance of the ordained with the faithful as agents of the evangelization of culture will move according to the rhythms of holy wisdom. An informed faith and an active love in the faithful will arise from authentic proclamation and vibrant preaching. Likewise, the joys and satisfactions of pastors will flow from the enthusiastic and creative apostolic action of the faithful who are in their pastoral care.

BUILDING A SYMBOLIC WORLD

We began this reflection on the common priesthood by wondering why the theology of the priesthood of the faithful, although central to the mystery of the Christian life, is not better known and has not been more thoroughly explored until now. There is no question about the authenticity or the importance of the teaching. It is simply a matter of unfamiliarity, of lacking the connecting ideas to link this treasure of Christian revelation to the experience of the faithful. The task of this book has been to understand the meaning and dynamics of the doctrine of the priesthood of the baptized and to investigate its significance for the lives of believers today. I will not try to summarize here everything that we have touched upon. Rather, I just want to highlight several aspects of baptismal priesthood that have the greatest potential to enrich the lives of believers.

During the writing of this book, I have kept in the forefront of my mind the predicament of persons whose lives are marked by suffering, great patience, and tragedy. It is one thing to hold a pious *idea* of suffering and an elevated *notion* of linking it to the sufferings of Christ; it may be quite another to experience the inescapable drudgery and exhaustion caused by long-term pain, sadness, anger, and incomprehension. Those who suffer the most, I think, are those who hold a visceral conviction of their suffering's essential lack of meaning.

On the other hand, when believers are guided through their suffering by the Holy Spirit and supported by fraternal love in the church, their baptismal priesthood is the redeeming comfort of their painful lives. I am confident it will be good news to them that they may participate in Christ's priesthood by directing their suffering as intentional love to complete "what is lacking in Christ's afflictions for the sake of his body, that is, the Church. . . ." (Col 1:24) Furthermore, I hope that these faithful people whose lives are penetrated with suffering and who find in their baptismal priesthood a key to meaning and spiritual contentment will testify to their experience and help others in the church to understand redemptive suffering. Their witness to their experience of this costly grace will be precious to the church, and we need to hear from them.

In addition, I have thought much about those at the age of enthusiasm, namely the youth and young adults. In general, youth is a time for the earnest pursuit of life, a time of dreams and hopes. As Erik Erikson and other developmental psychologists have clearly shown, there is characteristically a lovely altruism and a lofty idealism running through the hopefulness of the young.[23] For them especially, I want the meaning of the Christian life to be clearer and more alluring. Too many idealistic dreams end in defeat and cynicism precisely because youth find no clear articulation of the possibilities for vitality and creativity in a genuine Christian life. Baptismal priesthood is a call to partnering with God in the work of the new creation. Calling upon the energies of youth and young adults as stewards of the church's ministry can help to foster something that many of our parishes lack: the interplay of generations.

At the beginning of this chapter, we used the word "symbolic" to mean "having the quality of binding together grace and the commonplace." Even though we pray every day, "Give us this day our daily bread," we tend to miss the reality of divine gifts in the ordinary. The theology of baptismal priesthood shows us that, for those who are convinced disciples of Christ, human authenticity and holiness are inseparable. The spirituality of baptismal priesthood is the spirituality of a "symbolic" world, a world penetrated with grace. This penetration of the spiritual into the ordinary leads us to the determination to find strength, forgiveness, insight, and love in the untidy working out of each day's available reality. A symbolic life is also an intentional life. When we live Christ's priesthood as the "realized mystery" of the eucharistic Body of Christ, we find meaning and joy in offering ourselves every day as fully as we can.

Finally, the theology of the common priesthood illuminates for us the persistent love of God, who chooses to leave open the gates of mercy throughout the centuries so that we too may enter the paschal journey of Jesus and share in his work "to reconcile to himself all things, whether on earth or in heaven, by making peace through the blood of his cross" (Col 1:20).

The potential fruit of the common priesthood in action is easy to imagine, starting in the parish and flowing outward to the whole world. In parishes, the catechesis of the priesthood of the faithful could transform Sunday preaching, foster true participation in the celebration of the Eucharist, shape the goals of adult faith formation, and offer strength and dignity to families as they strive to develop "the domestic church." As the domestic church, couples and families will find all their natural inclinations toward harmony, friendship, and mutual service being drawn into the expression of the gifts of the Holy Spirit. This grace promotes the family's unity and contributes to the unity of the Body of Christ that is the parish.

The strength and clarity derived from learning about baptismal priesthood in the parish and living it at home will enable us to go forth to be a living sign of Christ's reconciling grace in the midst of our busy, work-a-day lives. In this way we will be God's instruments in bringing about the exact effect which the grace of baptism and Eucharist seeks to achieve: God's kingdom of justice and peace in the church, home, marketplace, and world. In short, the theology of baptismal priesthood penetrates every dimension of human experience. Everywhere we find both its rigorous demands and its joyful promise.

OUR GREATEST DIGNITY

"It is no longer I who live, but it is Christ who lives in me" (Gal 2:20). In this, as in other passages of the letters of Saint Paul, we can feel his overwhelming gratitude and humility. Paul, this great witness to the faith who is the Church's first great theologian, was once a fierce opponent and enemy of Christ. He then became the great evangelizer who pushed open the frontiers of the apostolic church. Paul insisted on the central mystery that the lives of the faithful become one life, one consecrated reality with Christ who is both God and human, both Lord and brother of us all. Christ's great sacrifice, precious beyond imagination, was to offer his own life in the flesh, through cruel suffering, humiliation, and painful death, as the bridge across our sin and mortality to eternal communion with God.

Paul discovered our oneness, our grafting into this new life of Christ. This mystery changes all the parameters of what it means to be human. Paul spelled out for his new churches the core meaning of their lives. They, who were often poor, displaced and marginal members of the great cities of the Mediterranean basin, were invited to become members of the Body of Christ, that is, invited into fellowship with God. In Paul's strange and moving language: "For while we live, we are always being given up to death for Jesus' sake, so that the life of Jesus may be made visible in our mortal flesh" (2 Cor 4:11).

The incalculable mercy of this mystery was Christ's absolute self-donation in the service of our salvation: "May I never boast of anything except the cross of our Lord Jesus Christ, by which the world has been crucified to me, and I to the world" (Gal 6:14). Paul's essential catechesis for the new churches entails explaining that we can never understand the real purpose of our existence without giving ourselves over completely to this new life in Christ. It is our greatest dignity and our only hope. Paul's intuition about our new identity as members of the Body of Christ is the foundation of the theology of baptismal priesthood. The great mercy for our lives is to enter already during our lifetime into a communion with God that will be the foundation of our "eternal life."

The priesthood of Christ is at the heart of this mercy: "It is Christ Jesus, who died, yes, who was raised, who is at the right hand of God, who intercedes for us" (Rom 8:34). Our hardships, our distress, our persecution, and any other toil or pain lived in union with Christ our Head are linked, by our priestly dignity, to the Lord's own project of giving glory to God and transforming the face of the earth. The mercy is that we have been made part of this reality that is the meaning and future of the world. The mercy is that everything that is otherwise unbearable in our lives becomes holy in union with the sacrifice of the Lord. The mercy is that we, as members of Christ, have the privilege of striving to bring about the freedom and fullness of the creation. The mercy is that his love embraces us in our weakness and in the concrete details of our ordinary lives.

The joy of our priesthood as Christ's faithful people is summed up in Paul's shout of exaltation: "We are more than conquerors through him who loved us. For I am convinced that neither death, nor life, nor angels, nor rulers, nor things present, nor things to come, nor powers, nor height, nor depth, nor anything else in all creation, will be able to separate us from the love of God in Christ Jesus our Lord" (Rom 8:37-39).

A living church is a church awake to the dynamic significance of its baptismal vocation, one eager for the investment of its members' lives in the transforming grace of Christ in the world, and one that offers itself as a sacrament—a living sign—of the real meaning of human life. A living church is a priestly people "who consecrate the world itself to God" (LG n. 34).

Notes

1. W. A. Carter, *Alex Carter: A Canadian Bishop's Memoirs* (North Bay, Ontario: Tomiko Publications, 1994) 50–51. Bishop Carter calls this message the pope's "Last Will and Testament," saying that "[a]s a matter of fact that was his last public audience."

2. Ibid., 50.

3. See Paul J. Philibert, "Symbolic and Diabolic Images of God," *Studies in Formative Spirituality* 6:1 (Feb. 1985) 87–101.

4. Marx's concept of alienation is treated in a great many works. I find especially helpful the chapter, "Religion and Alienation," in Peter L. Berger, *The Sacred Canopy: Elements of a Sociological Theory of Religion* (Garden City, NY: Doubleday, 1967) 81–101.

5. U.S. Bishops' Meeting, "Popular Devotional Practices: Basic Questions and Answers," *Origins* 33:25 (Nov. 27, 2003) 425–33.

6. Ibid., 428.

7. For a consideration of the importance of Christian ritual in children's lives, see P. J. Philibert, "Landscaping the Religious Imagination" in E. Bernstein and J. Brooks-Leonard, eds., *Children in the Assembly of the Church* (Chicago: Liturgical Training Publications, 1992) 10–29.

8. See the still useful review of this question in Yves Congar, *Lay People in the Church* (Westminster, MD: Newman Press, 1957) ch. V, esp. 346–76.

9. See the "Dogmatic Constitution on the Church," n. 1; and the "Pastoral Constitution on the Church in the Modern World," n. 1.

10. The strongest official affirmation of this view is found in the Apostolic Exhortation of Paul VI, "On Evangelization in the Modern World: *Evangelii Nuntiandi*," n. 14: "We wish to confirm once more that the task of evangelizing all peoples constitutes the essential mission of the church." Also note n. 15: "The church is an evangelizer, but she begins by being evangelized."

11. See G. Alberigo and J. Komonchak, eds., *History of Vatican II*, vol. III (Maryknoll, NY: Orbis, 2000). References to the "Decree on the Apostolate of Lay People: *Apostolicam Actuositatem*" from A. Flannery, ed., *Vatican II: Constitutions, Decrees, and Declarations* (Northport, NY: Costello, 1966) are abbreviated as AA in the text here.

12. Eight Vatican Offices, "Some Questions Regarding Collaboration of Nonordained Faithful in Priests' Sacred Ministry," *Origins* 27:24 (Nov. 27, 1997) 397–409. A number of the orientations of the 1997 Instruction are recapitulated in the 2004 Instruction, *"Redemptionis Sacramentum."*

13. Ibid., 403 (art. 1, n. 2). For the U.S. Bishops' position on LEMs, see *Lay Ecclesial Ministry: The State of the Question, A Report of the Subcommittee on Lay Ministry* (Washington, DC: National Conference of Catholic Bishops, 1999); also *Together in God's Service: Toward a Theology of Ecclesial Lay Ministry* (Washington, DC: National Conference of Catholic Bishops, 1998).

14. "Some Questions," op. cit., 402.

15. Ibid.

16. Susan K. Wood, "Conclusion: Convergence Points toward a Theology of Ordered Ministries," in Susan K. Wood, ed., *Ordering the Baptismal Priesthood: Theologies of Lay and Ordained Ministry* (Collegeville: The Liturgical Press, 2003) 256.

17. Ibid., 257.

18. Ibid., 259.

19. John Paul II, "Apostolic Exhortation, *Pastores Gregis*," *Origins* 33:22 (Nov. 6, 2003) 360. Note that the English translation uses *perichoresis* in n. 10, as we have seen. However, the official Latin text of *Pastores Gregis* uses the descriptive expression *motus circularis* in n. 10, although it too employs *perichoresis* in the sense noted here in n. 57.

20. William J. Hill, *The Three-Personed God: The Trinity as a Mystery of Salvation* (Washington, DC: The Catholic University of America Press, 1982) 272. A very helpful source for understanding contemporary developments in Trinitarian theology is Anne Hunt, *The Trinity and the Paschal Mystery: A Development in Re-*

cent Catholic Theology, New Theology Studies, No. 5 (Collegeville: The Liturgical Press, 1997).

21. *"Pastores Gregis,"* op. cit., n. 10.

22. Ibid.

23. A correlation of Eriksonian developmental psychology with growth in faith can be found in Paul J. Philibert, "Readiness for Ritual: Psychological Aspects of Maturity in Christian Celebration," in Regis A. Duffy, ed., *Alternative Futures for Worship,* vol. I, General Introduction (Collegeville: The Liturgical Press, 1987) 63–121.

Appendix A

Graced Sign
and Realized Mystery

Catholic sacramental theology is rooted in a basic principle that is clear in the witness of the New Testament. The incarnation of the Son of God in Jesus of Nazareth is the source of the church's spiritual power. As Scripture puts it, this divine Word has become flesh and dwelt among us (John 1:14); those who have looked upon him, have looked upon his Father (John 14:9); he remains in the church as the source from which all sanctification and ministry arise: "I am with you always, to the end of the age" (Matt 28:20).

In the middle of the last century, it became more common to refer to the Lord Jesus Christ himself as the primordial sacrament or holy sign through which God becomes present to us. His body as sign achieves what it signifies (the essential meaning of sacrament); namely, it allows us to meet God by encountering his humanity in Christ. When Christ invites us to discipleship in calling us to "come, follow" him, he likewise invites us to learn to be like him and become transformed (Matt 10; Phil 2).

A complementary principle comes to us from the epistles of St. Paul in which the faithful are described as baptized into Christ's Body, becoming members of a new creation that makes them one with Christ who is their head. This is the basis for naming the church as the basic sacrament of salvation, such as we see in LG n. 1 and in various passages of the Catechism. The members of Christ's Body receive spiritual gifts and charisms to enable and fortify them to represent Christ, and they are moved in this way by the Holy Spirit to accomplish God's purposes.

This transformation of the faithful into dynamic expressions of Christ's spiritual power is the objective of the Christian life. In the text of this book, we have consistently referred to this dimension as the "realized mystery" of the Eucharist. By eating the eucharistic Body of Christ, the faithful are given the grace to become themselves his Mystical Body. This too can be explained in terms of the Scriptures.

As we noted in chapters 5 and 8, there are two distinct strands of witness to the institution of the Eucharist. In the Synoptic Gospels, the so-called words of institution are pronounced by Jesus in the Upper Room: "Take, eat; this is my body . . ." and "Do this in memory of me" (Matt 26:26–29; Mark 14:22–25; Luke 22:17–19; 1 Cor 11:23–26). But the Gospel of John replaces the words of institution with the washing of the disciples' feet in chapter 13, followed by the exhortation of the Lord, "So if I, your Lord and Teacher, have washed your feet, you also ought to wash one another's feet. For I have set you an example, that you also should do as I have done to you" (John 13:14).

These two different New Testament accounts are parallel expressions of the two dimensions of the eucharistic mystery. The synoptic institution narratives point to the eucharistic body of the Lord, whereas the footwashing in John points toward the exemplary symbolism of the Lord acting in his Mystical Body. The faithful, following his example, realize—i.e., make actual—the mystery of the Eucharist by representing Christ and acting as expressive members of his priestly body.

In this book, we have used the term "graced sign" to refer to the transubstantiated eucharistic bread, which is at once both "graced"—that is, really changed into Christ's body—and a "sign," that is, a material dimension that points beyond itself to the spiritual mystery of the new creation. Likewise, we have used the term "realized mystery" to refer to the ecclesial community, the members of which have become, through their mutual love and shared ministry, the living sacrament of Christ alive in his church. The bread of Life transforms the faithful into a spiritually powerful healing community.

There is a long history of the use of such language, which makes the distinction between the Eucharist as a means of sanctification and transformation, on the one hand, and the Eucharist as the objective and end of the church's sacramental life, on the other hand. It will be worthwhile to point out some landmarks in this rich tradition. This will help to explain the language I have been using throughout this book; it will also deepen our understanding of what is at issue in terms of the Eucharist as "realized mystery."

FROM ST. AUGUSTINE TO ST. THOMAS AQUINAS

From the Christian tradition before him, St. Augustine (353–430) received a clear teaching that the Eucharist had these two dimensions: one external and visible, which is the transformed bread blessed by Christ's words; the other internal and invisible, which is the power of the Holy Spirit producing the grace of a deeper relationship with Christ in those who eat it. Augustine used the word *sacrament* to indicate the sacred sign that signifies a spiritual reality of which it is the image. By signifying it, the sacrament brings the spiritual reality into being. Thus, with Augustine, the term *sign* takes on an effective or causal power not ordinarily associated with the idea of sign as it is commonly used today.

Just as the body of the Incarnate Son is a living sign of God present within him and acting through his words and gestures, so also is the eucharistic bread a sign of Christ really present to those who receive him in faith and in the power of the Holy Spirit. "The power inherent in the sacrament, then, brings to bear upon the recipient[s]—provided [they] are suitably disposed—the sanctifying work of Christ or of the Holy Spirit."[1] In consuming the sacrament of his Body and Blood, they truly receive him into themselves and are changed by the power of this divine nourishment.

A further contribution of Augustine's teaching is his insistence upon the fact that Christ is both the author and the objective of all the sacraments. This means that the supernatural reality which the sacramental sign both signifies and causes to come into being is not merely the sanctification of the individual recipients of sacramental grace, but the communion of all the members of Christ's Body in the "whole Christ," head and members, together alive in the power of the Holy Spirit.

St. Thomas Aquinas (1224–1274) made this same distinction between the two dimensions of the Eucharist perfectly clear in his writings. It is his understanding of the mystery of the Eucharist that I aim to express in my use of the terms "graced sign" and "realized mystery." The consecrated bread and wine are the Body and Blood of Christ really present to us in the form of and through the causality of a "graced sign," namely, eating and drinking the bread and wine over which Christ's words have been pronounced by an ordained leader. We eat and drink in obedience to Christ's command: "Take and eat; . . . take and drink . . ." In St. Thomas's thinking, just as the humanity of Christ was the instrument through which God brought about our salvation, so too eating the bread and wine, conjoined with the words of Christ and the invocation of the Holy Spirit, are the instruments that bring about our communion in the Body of Christ and all the spiritual effects that flow from that communion. Our inhering as members in the one body of Christ is the "realized mystery" of the Eucharist.[2]

Holy Scripture, the writings of the theologians of the early church, and medieval theology all emphasized particularly this "realized mystery." This presence of Christ in our hearts and the communion that it achieves among those who receive him is brought about through the means of the sacred bread. This requires the real presence of Christ in the transubstantiated bread and wine. Yet the emphasis falls not so much upon the "graced sign" as real presence, but upon the *purpose* of this presence, which is the presence of Christ *in us.*

After the Protestant Reformation and the Council of Trent, "the [realized mystery] was pushed into the background, while the [graced sign], that is, the real presence in the sacred host, was emphasized so much that it seemed to be an end in itself . . ."[3] For centuries, the eucharistic sacrament was adored, but no longer eaten by the faithful. As a result, the priestly action of the faithful—their heartfelt offering of the spiritual sacrifices of their own lives and actions along with the sacrifice of Christ, their head—became either something completely unknown to them or something detached from the celebration of the Eucharist. The "graced sign" of eating the Body of the Lord is for the sake of the "realized mystery" of lives that can become living signs of Christ's sanctifying presence in ordinary human life.

EUCHARIST AND THE PRIESTHOOD OF THE FAITHFUL

Our participation in Christ's priesthood through baptism is God's gift to the faithful. It can be thought of as the reformulation of the very meaning of our lives.[4] Christ's priesthood touches us at the very core of our being where we make ongoing contact with the divine source of our life. His priesthood penetrates every dimension of our being and of our experience in order to direct them toward God. As a consequence, through the common priesthood, all our vital powers—

from the instant of their arising at the center of our life—are given meaning by being directed to God.

The realization of this mystery allows us to see that our participation in Christ's priesthood through baptismal grace constitutes the very nature of Christian existence. In other words, a Christian life necessarily has a priestly character. The common priesthood links our lives, as projects intentionally offered in obedience and sacrifice to God, together with Christ's own obedience and self-immolation. We offer ourselves along with Christ as he offers himself to God his Father in the heavenly ministry that constitutes his own unique priesthood. As we saw in chapters 5 and 7, the common priesthood of the faithful is actualized in all the acts and intentions of ordinary life, and is something repeatedly affirmed by the solemn teaching of Vatican II (cf. SC 6, 7; LG 33-34).

In this respect, the participation of the ordained (bishops, priests, deacons) in the common priesthood—the transforming intentionality of the whole of life as an oblation of love and obedience joined to Christ's own self-oblation—does not differ with respect to the "realized mystery" of the Eucharist from that of the other faithful. There is only one *totus Christus* (whole Christ) embracing all the baptized, ordained or not ordained, as members joined to the one divine head of the Mystical Body. This, of course, is why the word *common* in this context means "shared." The privilege of being integrated into Christ's priestly ministry in the presence of his Father is common to the sacred ministers who are ordained and to the faithful whom they serve in their ministries of preaching, guiding, and presiding in worship.

These latter ministries—the prophetic, royal, and priestly services offered to the faithful by the ordained—are exercised as expressions of the "graced sign" of Christ living in the church as the means of salvation and of our communion with God. As a consequence of this compassionate, efficacious ministry of the ordained, the faithful receive holy gifts that mediate their self-offering and their spiritual transformation, making them the Body of Christ (along with their pastors), the "realized mystery" of the Eucharist, and themselves a source of sanctification for the world (cf. LG n. 34). Of them all, Christ says, "I came out that [you] may have life, and have it abundantly" (John 10:10); and "Those who abide in me and I in them bear much fruit . . ." (John 15:5).

Notes

1. David Bourke, "Introduction" in St. Thomas Aquinas, *Summa Theologiae*, vol. 56 (3a, 60–65) *The Sacraments* (New York: McGraw-Hill, 1975) xvi.

2. *Summa Theologiae*, 3a 66, 1, where Aquinas uses the Latin phrase *res et sacramentum* to designate what I have called the "graced sign," and the phrase *res tantum* to designate what I have called the "realized mystery." For an extended discussion of the development of this kind of terminology for the Eucharist, see Edward J. Kilmartin (ed. Robert J. Daly), *The Eucharist in the West: History and Theology* (Collegeville: The Liturgical Press, 1998) esp. 47, 62–67, 118–26.

3. Edward Schillebeeckx, "Transubstantiation, Transfinalization, Transignification" in R. Kevin Seasoltz, ed., *Living Bread, Saving Cup: Readings on the Eucharist* (Collegeville: The Liturgical Press, 1987) 187. See also the magisterial summary of this question in Yves Congar, *Un peuple messianique: salut et libération* (Paris: Editions du Cerf, 1975) esp. 57–74.

4. See the "Postface" by M.-J. Nicolas in Marie de la Trinité, *Filiation et sacerdoce des chrétiens* (Paris: Editions Lethielleux, 1986) 183; see also 137–41 for key texts of the author.

An Open Letter to Religious

In the Decree on the Appropriate Renewal of Religious Life, Vatican II proposed two general principles for renewal. The first was the return to the gospel inspiration of religious life, seeking to understand the following of Christ as the call to which religious life responds. The second was the renovation of the institute through a return to the original inspiration of the founder and to the charism of the institute as it evolved through its history.

In the U.S., a great deal of energy was applied to responding to the rediscovery of the charisms of our institutes. This involved historical research, chapters and assemblies, and articles and monographs interpreting the implications of the institute's founding purposes and charism for the life of religious in the present day. The result was the rediscovery of the core meaning of the institute's contribution to the life of the church and often a burst of pride in the past achievements of the religious family. For some religious, this process of renewal amounted to a kind of re-founding in the sense of re-grounding and revivification. This became for many a kind of rebirth in the sense that religious rediscovered in a fresh way the evangelical inspiration, the generosity and compassion of their founders, and the living expression of this charism in their contemporary experience.

The study of the scriptural foundations of religious life was also substantial. Some notable and influential examples of this were books in North America by Thomas Dubay, Roger Tillard, and Sandra Schneiders. In addition, some of the greatest theologians of the post-Vatican II epoch undertook to contribute to the theology of religious life: I think of writing, for example, by Karl Rahner, Edward Schillebeeckx, and Johannes Metz. However, these studies failed to attend to an important contribution of theologian Yves Congar, who suggested in 1950 that there is a special significance of the common priesthood for religious. In his now classic *Lay People in the Church*, Congar remarked that religious life creates the conditions for an intense and exemplary realization of the common priesthood of the faithful. I believe that Congar's intuition is so important that I want to elaborate upon it here.

As we have seen throughout this book, the heart of the common priesthood is the willing and intentional self-offering of the faithful in a way that embraces the whole of their lives as spiritual sacrifices united with the priestly self-gift of Christ to his Father. Awakening to the significance of our integration into Christ's priesthood through our baptismal consecration, we come to appreciate how the whole of life is linked to the mystery of Christ. As Congar noted, the nature of religious life is such as to keep its members in constant touch with the word of God, to create daily regular occasions to respond to God's word in praise and thanksgiving, and to live within the world in the same spirit of poverty and self-giving service as did Christ.

In other words, common prayer structures the day of religious, especially for institutes who observe the choral celebration of the Liturgy of the Hours, so as to constantly renew the dialogue between the faithful and the Word of God. Other elements of the celebration of God's Word include *lectio divina*, study, and preaching (and preparation for preaching)—all exercises that reshape people's frame of reference by leading them to submit their own interests to the demands of the living Word of God. Further, the environment of the religious house creates many reminders of our rootedness in the mystery of Christ. In fact, the shared environment of the monastery or religious house is an expression of the common faith that both enriches all the members and likewise expresses their shared spirit and traditions. Making their corporate existence visible and effective in the social life of the community is at the heart of religious life.

Too often religious life has been understood juridically and without sufficient theological insight. Many lay faithful still imagine that the meaning of religious life is the renunciation of money, sex, and power understood as a difficult sacrifice of human goods in order to enter into a religious world that has ecclesiastical prestige, but little in common with the ordinary concerns of families or of the wider world. Such a misunderstanding reduces the possibilities for the prophetic link between religious and the parish life around them. The fundamental sociological dynamic of religious life is not separation, but solidarity. To see how this is the case, I will try to explain how the vows express dynamics common to the following of Christ offered to all the faithful.

Congar's great insight was to push all these questions to a greater depth by explaining that for all the faithful, their entering into solidarity with Christ's priestly self-offering is the fundamental element in their following of Christ. This insight provides a shift of perspective in looking at the vows of religious. The vows are not ends in themselves; rather, they are means to render believers more deeply integrated into their participation in Christ's priesthood. This opens up new meaning for the practice of religious life.

The vowed poverty of religious is not only a rare, juridical exercise concerning judgments about sums of money or salaries and their destination. It is also, and more importantly, a dimension of daily experience and ordinary decisions. The vow of poverty commits the religious to interpret his or her life in the light of Christ's example of poverty which Philippians 2 describes as a *kenosis*—a setting aside of the divine Son's privileges as equal to the Father. As Philippians 2:10 puts it: "[H]ave that mind in you that was in Christ Jesus," meaning that the faithful are exhorted to adopt the spirit of *kenosis* in the circumstances of their lives and see themselves linked to Christ's own self-offering as they lovingly submit to God's call.

Life in religious community normally provides frequent opportunities for brothers and sisters to abandon their individual preferences out of a fundamental choice to live a deeper life of unity in the Body of Christ, what we have frequently referred to as the "realized mystery" of the Eucharist. Voluntary poverty becomes the instrument for the intentional preference for the sacrament of a common life in the Body of Christ over the pursuit of one's self-centered concerns. Voluntary poverty is a very challenging practice, and often leads to pain and suffering.

The intentional acceptance of this suffering for the sake of realizing a living sign of the Body of Christ is the most common and, perhaps, the most important expression of religious poverty. However, the theological understanding of this kind of poverty as a willing solidarity with Christ in following him on the path to real life transports the whole question of poverty beyond matters of material goods and relocates the question within the very heart of the following of

Christ. It is a joy and a privilege to be allowed to share in Christ's own *kenosis*, precisely for the sake of generating life in others by means of our setting aside our own willfulness and self-interests.

Religious chastity, expressed in terms of voluntary celibacy, is very difficult for many in our culture to understand. It is part of being human to want to appear attractive and beloved to another. North American consumer culture thrives on stimulating sexual drives in the service of selling goods. This commercial concupiscence is so pervasive, in fact, that we swim in a bath of sensuous images reaching out to us from billboards, magazine ads, TV commercials, and Internet spam, to mention a few. Even contemplative monasteries have to defend their enclosure from the invasiveness of pornography and materialism on the Internet.

Chastity can only work when it is married to growth in prayer. Chastity can never be a refusal of love, only a commitment to growth in love. The object of that love is the "whole Christ," the head and all his members. On both sides of this quest for Christian love—the movement toward Christ as our head and the movement toward the members of his Body—the development of mature understanding and practices is difficult and often painful. The prayer of the chaste, loving Christian is the endlessly repeated gift of the self in generous imitation of Christ before his Father and of our religious founders before their Lord. Prayer finally leads the faithful to a level of hopeful self-giving so simple that it cannot be put into words; it can only be lived in trust.

When the person is grounded and renewed in this kind of prayer, he or she is implicated in a relation to everyone else. No more than Christ ever turned away in revulsion from those who crossed his path, can we spurn those who become a part of our lives. Our chastity has a fundamental, positive side: it is a commitment to others out of love for Christ who is becoming the affective center of our own lives. It is love for others in and with Christ. This seemingly impossible and unrealistic transformation of Christians is not something that can be explained reasonably; it can only be lived. Further, to try to live the negative side of religious chastity, the renunciation of sexual gratification and of a family, without this positive dimension is both pointless and probably impossible.

The vow of chastity is thereby linked to Christ's priestly gift of himself for the sake of the little and the lost. Christ's heavenly ministry as a priest seeks to draw those who belong to him into the unity that he has with the Father. "As the Father has loved me, so I have loved you; abide in my love" (John 15:9). The human affectivity of the disciple comes to be shaped after the example of the Master. Our powers of human love grow in freedom and in scope so as to draw others into real unity with the Lord who is becoming the center of our own affections. Our common priesthood is exercised through chastity with simplicity, purity, and energy that can become graced expressions of Christ's own hunger for the unity of the human family.

Obedience is the vow that many religious themselves find the most difficult to understand and to live. The submission of one person's will to another can appear a moral self-mutilation in a society in which so much passion is expended in seeking power over others. The consumer culture demeans filial relationships, as is evident in the ways in which TV caricatures the lost authority of parents in sit-com families. The idea that someone through loving service might become a sacrament of fatherly or motherly care for a spiritual family has all but disappeared from our lexicon of explanations for obedience.

Much of great value has been written in recent years on the meaning of religious obedience. I will only mention two points here.

First, religious obedience is a communal virtue. The whole community has pledged itself to listen to the proclaimed word of God and to obey. By listening together—and listening to one another listen, as religious do in chapter, for example—we move closer to one another as pilgrims on a common journey toward the promise proclaimed to us in God's word. Without this context of a faithful community, submission of members to a leader loses its theological significance.

Second, when religious obedience is indeed rooted in a community alive in God's word, the willing response to a call to mission and service from a religious superior and from the community is a true living sacrament of Christ's own obedience. Obedience that is free, joyful, and creative—that calls persons out of themselves into risks that become fruitful for corporate life, that pushes individuals into new episodes of generosity and generativity—that kind of obedience is really a sign of the kingdom of God. It can only arise out of the following of Christ.

And now I must say something that pertains to the explanation of all three vows. The kind of self-emptying, love, and generativity that I have been describing are not charisms reserved in the church for religious alone. Indeed, this is the point. Religious, in undertaking a life that shapes and structures the way they live in order to offer models and incentives to the faithful, find profound meaning not only in their own continuing configuration to their Master, but in their generous commitment to this form of life precisely because it is illustrative and generative for the church as a whole.

From this comes the importance of the spiritual hospitality of religious who open up their environments of reflective beauty and their times of common prayer to the faithful. Many of the faithful want to share life with religious and learn from them the spirit of Christ's poverty, chastity, and obedience as it is lived in the tradition of their institutes.

Congar's insight was that religious are bound to find this understanding of their ecclesial lives more meaningful than a purely juridical interpretation of their vows. Religious who understand that their life is plunged deeply into the mystery of Christ's priesthood become a source of joy and a call to growth for others. Their life is always fruitful. It is a path of discipleship that leads religious into a personal configuration to their Master. But this same path also opens opportunities for others to recognize and realize the meaning of the Gospel that the church proclaims. It provides comradeship for those who are fearful or unsure.

This theme deserves a fuller treatment than would be appropriate here. But I want to suggest to religious another way to read what we have done in this book. It is an invitation to them to see the very purpose of their ecclesial vocation in the light of the fundamental mystery of their baptismal integration into the priesthood of Christ.

Index of Names

Aquinas, St. Thomas, 32, 97–98, 106, 123–24, 160–61
Augustine, St., 54, 55, 158

Baldovin, John F., 92
Balthasar, Hans Urs von, 55, 73
Baumbach, Gerard, 22, 38
Bedford, Nancy, 13
Bourgeois, Daniel, 45, 55, 73, 145
Bourke, David, 163

Calvin, John, 75, 92
Cassian, John, 125–26, 131
Castrillon Hoyos, Cardinal Dario, 144
Chenu, M.-D., 73
Congar, Yves, vii, 19, 56–59, 73, 75, 82, 92, 163, 165, 169
Corbon, Jean, 38, 43, 48, 55
Curry, Bishop Thomas, 14
Cyril of Jerusalem, St., 23, 33, 38

Daly, Robert, 69, 73
D'Antonio, William, 7, 20
Davidson, James, 10–11, 14, 20
Dubay, Thomas, 162
Duquoc, Christian, 31, 38

Erikson, Erik, 152, 157

Ernst, Cornelius, 55

Froehle, Bryan, 20

Galileo, 82
Greeley, Andrew, 12
Guroian, Vigen, 33, 38

Hoge, Dean R., 20

Isaac, Abbot, 125–26

Jacob, François, 29
Jephthah (and his daughter), 115
John XXIII, Pope, 56–57
John Paul II, Pope, 43, 55, 66, 92, 97–99, 128, 148
Jungmann, Joseph, 58

Kilmartin, Edward J., 163

Luther, Martin, 2, 3

Maritain, Jacques, 77–79, 87, 91, 92
Marx, Karl, 136
Merton, Thomas, 86–87, 92, 108, 112
Meyendorff, John, 55
Muller, Jim, 16

Newman, John Henry, 84, 92, 133
Nicolas, M.-J., 163
Nouwen, Henri, 81, 92

O'Connor, Flannery, 33, 38
O'Malley, Archbishop Sean, 4, 20

Philibert, Paul, 38, 73, 157
Pius XI, Pope, 132
Putnam, Robert D., 92

Rahner, Karl, 164
Rauschenberg, Walter, 22, 38

Robinson, J.A.T., 20

Schillebeeckx, Edward, 45, 102, 163

Schiltz, Patrick, 15, 21
Schmemann, Alexander, 26, 38
Schneiders, Sandra, 164

Tillard, Roger, 164
Trungpa, Chögyam, 20

Ware, Kallistos, 28
Wood, Susan, 88, 146, 157

Index of Subjects

adult faith formation, 100–104, 134
advertising, 120
alienation, 136–37
attention, 123–24, 130
"available reality", 25, 153

Baptism, 22–26, 30, 35, 37, 48, 132
Baroque Catholicism, 78
Body of Christ, Theology of, 2, 19, 49

Catholic population in U.S., 6
Chalcedon, Council of, 43
charismatic renewal, 3
children, 140
clergy shortage, 7, 14, 134, 146
Confirmation, 33
consumer society, 99, 112

domestic church, 107, 140, 153

epiclesis, 33, 48–54, 62, 127
"essential difference", 144–45
exorcisms, 34

faith, 83–86
    notional and real, 84, 133
families, 100, 102, 107, 109
foreign-born priests, 6
freedom, 34–35

graced sign, 51, 65–66, 71, 95, 107, 109, 122, 129, 138, 145, 159–61

high places, 114
holiness, 104, 108
Humanae Vitae, 8, 16
"hymn" of Christ, 61–62

imagination, 133
    diabolic imagination, 133
    symbolic imagination, 133, 135, 151
immortality, 41
Incarnation, 42, 44–45, 129–30
intentionality, intention, 36, 120, 123, 127, 130, 152, 153, 162

kairos, 5, 8, 14, 15
kenosis, 42, 44, 67–68, 166–67
kingdom (Christ as King), 95–97

laity, 18, 63, 135, 137, 142–43
Latino (Hispanic) Americans, 12
Latino (Hispanic) priests, 21
Latino (Hispanic) Protestants, 12–14
Lay Ecclesial Ministers, 7–8, 88, 134, 142, 146–48
liturgy, liturgies, 61, 62, 141

Mass attendance, 8–9
mixed marriages, 9, 11
Mysteries of Christ, 24, 28, 30–34, 38

paschal mystery, 29–30, 47, 49, 52, 67, 83, 90, 153
Pastores Gregis, 148–51
perichoresis, 149–50
popular devotions, 138, 140
prayer, 104, 123, 167
   ceaseless (imageless) prayer, 124–25
   "little prayers", 111, 126
priesthood, 71–72, 119, 127–28, 132, 144
   baptismal priesthood, 59, 63, 119–20, 127, 129, 133, 137, 139, 141–42, 152
prophetic mission
   bishops and priests, 149
   faithful, 78, 83, 88–89, 142

real presence, 138, 161–62, 166
realized mystery, 52, 60, 62, 64–66, 71, 95, 107, 122, 128–29, 138, 145, 153, 159–62
revelation, 31, 33
rights of Catholics (Code of Canon Law), 18
"royal" mission, 97–98

sacrament(s), 24, 40, 44
   Jesus as sacrament, 40, 41, 44–46, 158
   Church as sacrament, 46, 158

Christian(s) as sacrament, 48, 49, 54
   seven sacraments, 47
sacrifices, 4, 69, 115, 123, 162
   animal sacrifice, 113–14, 118
   blood sacrifice, 115
   purification rituals, 116
sexual abuse crisis, 5, 15
Small Christian Communities, 80, 102–103, 140, 150
social capital, 89
Spirit, Holy, 32, 47–48, 51, 84, 86, 134, 153
spiritual friendship, 103
spiritual sacrifices, 63–64, 66, 69–71, 101, 119–20, 121–25, 127, 129, 131, 138, 161–62, 165
suffering, 68, 123, 152
Sunday Mass, 94, 101
symbolic matter, 51, 65, 71, 95, 109, 122

teens, 103–104
theosis (divinization), 49–50
transubstantiation(s), 48–49, 55
Trinity, Holy, 32, 42, 53, 68, 129, 148

vocation, 94
Voice of the Faithful, 5, 16, 21

water, 23
websites, 102–104

young adult Catholics, 9–10, 103–104